50 Literacy ACTIVITIES

for Your Kindergarten Classroom

Photographs: p. 4: Jenny Acheson; pp. 8, 9, 33, 43, 53: James Levin; p. 17: Susan Richman.
Illustrations: Rita Lascaro; Cover: Barbara Lipp; pp.6-7: Ellen Sasaki.

Copyright © 1997 by Scholastic Inc.
All rights reserved. Published by Scholastic Inc.
Printed in the U.S.A.
ISBN 0-590-29889-5

1 2 3 4 5 6 7 8 9 10   02 01 00 99 98 97

Contents

5 0   L i t e r a c y   A c t i v i t i e s

Introduction

LiteracyinAction

Kindergartners' desire to express themselves and understand their place in the world is the foundation for literacy development.

There's a soft buzz of voices hovering over the classroom. One child sits cross-legged on a cushion, leafing through the pages of a book, murmuring to herself. Two other children huddle together over a drawing, talking about the story they're composing and whether or not they will write "in script." Another child updates the weather chart — one of many signs posted around the room — to show that the rainy morning has turned into a sunny afternoon.

These kindergartners may be like those in your classroom: They are avid learners, curious about their world and eager to interact meaningfully and purposefully with it. Their growing literacy skills help them access new experiences and open doors to your classroom and beyond.

Your Role

As a kindergarten teacher, you've assumed a challenging role: to feed children's natural desire to learn as well as to prepare them for future academic success.

• By creating a literacy-rich environment, you can provide the organization, setting, activities, and materials to empower children to construct their own literacy learning.

• By balancing modeling, encouragement, and inspiration with instruction and open-ended questioning, you can help children achieve literacy skills that last a lifetime.

This book offers 50 developmentally appropriate language and literacy activities for kindergartners. They are organized by topic: Storytelling, Speaking and Listening, Letters and Sounds, Writing, and Making Books.

As you adapt the activities for your children, keep in mind that they are designed to be open-ended and can be combined with children's ongoing language and literacy explorations. Use the Literacy Setup on the following pages as a guide for great materials and equipment to create and enrich your home base for language and literacy activities.

Getting the most from the activity plans

The activity plan format is simple and easy to follow. Each plan includes most of the following:

AIM: the purpose of the activity: what children will do and learn.

MATERIALS: basic materials and special items to gather. You will find that you have most of these on hand. Others can be donated by parents or local businesses.

IN ADVANCE: tips for materials to prepare or arrangements to make before introducing the activity.

WARM-UP: ways to introduce the activity or underlying theme. Open-ended questions help children think critically and probe topics more deeply.

ACTIVITY: steps and suggestions for introducing materials, helping children get started, and guiding the activity.

REMEMBER: social/emotional, cultural, and developmental considerations; tips about ways to relate other skills and concepts to the activity theme; and occasional safety reminders.

OBSERVATIONS: ideas and strategies for observing children that will help you understand children's individual learning styles as well as help you guide, extend, or evaluate the activity.

SPIN-OFFS: ideas for extending the activity into different curriculum and skills areas.

BOOKS: children's books related to the activity or theme.

Colleagues, aides, student teachers, volunteers, and family members can all benefit from fun suggestions for child-centered language and literacy activities. So feel free to duplicate and share the plans for your program's use.

Literacy Setup

Teacher   Supplies

Aa Bb Cc Dd Ee Ff Gg Hh Ii Jj Kk Ll Mm Nn Oo Pp Qq Rr Ss Tt Uu Vv Ww Xx Yy Zz

The Three Bears

Whales

BUGS

William's Doll

Space   Animals   My Family   Fairy Tales

①

Our Names

Ana	Olivia
Brian	Pete
Betty	Rita
Erin	Simone
June	Tito
Jacob	Thomas
Lila	Victor
Maggie	Wendy
Michael	Yolanda

⑥

abcdef
ABCDEF

②

④

Photo Albums

Our Class Books

Our Journals

Ana

Pete

Lila

June

⑤

Our Class Books

Kids' Magazine

Nature magazine

③

1 A library filled with fiction and nonfiction books exposes children to real-world topics and the world of make-believe.

2 After a book is shared, children will enjoy being able to "read along" while listening to the story.

3 A soft rug and giant pillows make sharing a book with a friend a very pleasant experience.

4 Photos are a great way to spark conversation among children as they reminisce about past events.

5 Keep journals accessible to children so they can document events as they happen throughout the day.

6 An oversized name chart is a perfect example of meaningful environmental print in the classroom.

7 Books grouped by author help children become familiar with the style and interests of a particular writer.

8 A word-wall bulletin board is an ideal place for children to collect new words.

9 A well-stocked shelf of writing materials and bookmaking supplies invites children to experiment with language.

10 A small table provides space for children to create stories or write in their journals.

11 A well-supplied and colorfully displayed art center is a great place for creative expression.

12 Computers in the classroom offer children the opportunity to practice letter and word recognition.

Building
aLoveofLanguage

Your classroom holds a wealth of opportunities for children's oral and written language and explorations.

Children make connections between spoken and written language when you write their ideas. Verbalize what you are doing as you write letters and words.

The activities in this book are designed to encourage children to use literacy skills in all areas of your curriculum and all centers in your room. This integrated approach reinforces and helps to develop your children's language and literacy skills. It also shows your children how to apply these skills in everyday life — an essential element in encouraging independent, self-motivated readers and writers.

As you make use of the activity plans that follow, remember to:

- Include daily listening and responding to story and nonfiction books in order to provide key experience with the language found in literature and in real life.

- Provide and model diverse forms of written expression in your environment in order to help children build their ability to appreciate and interpret print.

- Offer a variety of magazines, newspapers, and other popular forms of print children can explore based on their individual abilities and interests.

- Encourage children to keep a notebook for daily journaling of drawings and emerging writings. Help them create their own ways of expressing their ideas and feelings, and offer regular practice in reading and writing in their own way.

Activity Plans
for
Storytelling

Kindergartners are natural storytellers. They use stories to interpret experi-ence and make meaning in their lives. They can create a story using a simple prop, an art material, or nothing at all.

Storytelling often gives shape to children's developing reading and writing skills. As they create and tell stories, children learn about the author's craft. Characterization, sequence and flow, and even word choice are elements of both oral and written story-telling experiences. As children create their group or individual stories, they use these language skills in ways that are interesting and functional for them.

Throughout the Day

■ Use story starters (such as "on my way to school" or "you won't believe what happened yesterday") when talking with children about special events. You'll be providing vocabulary models that children can use in their own storytelling.

■ It's been said that "every picture tells a story," so when children show their paint-ings, ask them if it has a story to tell!

■ Positively acknowledge children when they are telling stories. Note specific parts, such as the charac-ters, sequence, plot, and ending.

Around the Room

■ Provide flannel board stories in quiet areas of the room, such as the library area, dra-matic-play area, or even in a special "storytelling" area.

■ Place unusual storytelling props in the lis-tening area. Invite children to tape-record each other as they use the props to create their own stories. Make special prop boxes to help children retell favorite storybooks.

Dramatization opportunities spark excitement and build a love of language.

Tell a "Superlative" Story
Word play can be creative and fun.

Materials

- experience-chart paper
- markers
- tape recorder and audiocassette (optional)
- drawing paper
- crayons

Aim

Children will use expressive and receptive language skills as they experiment with new words and concepts.

Warm-Up

Gather together and ask, "What's the biggest thing you've ever seen? What's the tiniest thing you've ever seen?" Continue to ask open-ended questions that involve superlatives such as *brightest, darkest, highest,* and *lowest.*

Activity

1 After children have had time to play with words, begin to record their responses. What are the loudest things they can think of? The quietest? Encourage children to illustrate a few superlative/opposite combinations.

2 Explain that together you will create a pass-along story, in which you narrate and the group fills in details. (You might want to have a tape recorder on hand so you can transcribe the children's story into a book later.)

3 Start the story with "Once upon a time there was the ugliest (prettiest, fastest, etc.)...." Invite one child to decide what comes next and then tell something about it.

For example, one child might say, "Once upon a time there was the ugliest frog in the world and he liked to eat lots and lots of bugs." Use the superlatives on the experience chart for your story sentences. Continue the story, using another superlative word: "The ugliest frog who lived in the biggest...." Invite another child to complete that line.

4 Eventually children will start to suggest superlatives themselves. Write the finished story on the bottom of separate sheets of paper so each child can illustrate the section he or she added. Put the sheets together to create a superlative storybook.

Remember

- When children play with language, they are constructing their own knowledge about how words work in speech, writing, and reading.

Observations

During the next few days, note how children use superlatives in their language and play.

Books

Share these superlative books.
- *The Biggest House in the World* by Leo Lionni (Pantheon Books)
- *The Little Fish That Got Away* by Bernadine Cook (Scholastic Inc.)

SPIN-OFFS

- Try making a list of superlatives at group time, when you have a little free time between activities, or even when children are waiting in line! Children might pick a favorite superlative of the day and explore how many things they can describe with it.

Orchestrate a Story
Here's a way to combine music and language.

Materials

- repetitive story that features several characters
- rhythm instruments such as triangles, tambourines, bells, and wooden sticks
- chart paper
- markers

Aim

Children will use active listening and speaking skills as they "play along" with a familiar story.

Warm-Up

Read or tell the story you've chosen to children. Discuss the different characters and what they do, paying attention to their specific traits: big or small, young or old, friendly or scary. Record the character names and their traits on chart paper. Introduce the collection of rhythm instruments. Give children time to play with them and to listen to the different sounds they make.

Activity

1 Invite children to help you retell the story using the rhythm instruments for sound effects and characterizations. Use your chart to review each character's traits.

2 Ask children to choose a rhythm instrument that sounds like a character. For example, in *The Three Billy Goats Gruff*, the biggest goat might be represented by a drum and the smallest by a bell. Draw a simple outline of the instrument chosen for each character next to the character's name on the chart.

3 Let each child choose a character to "play" on a rhythm instrument. If there are more children than characters, invite other children to make sound effects.

4 Retell the story, pausing to name characters or actions so that children can chime in. Repeat the activity, inviting children to trade instruments.

Remember

- Emphasize that creativity is more important than perfect orchestration of words and instruments.

Observations

- How is children's sense of timing and rhythm developing? Do they realize when to start and stop playing their instruments?

Books

Try orchestrating these versions of old favorites.
- *The House That Jack Built* by Paul Galdone (McGraw-Hill)
- *The Little Old Lady Who Wasn't Afraid of Anything* by Linda Williams (HarperCollins)
- *The Three Billy Goats Gruff* by Peter Christian Asbjorsen (Harcourt Brace Jovanovich)

SPIN-OFFS

- Place the rhythm instruments where small groups of children can use them to dramatize stories themselves or with puppets.

Monster Mountain

A story can lead to a fanciful flight.

Materials

- recording of "flying" music (such as from *Peter Pan*)
- box or large hollow or foam block
- *Where the Wild Things Are* by Maurice Sendak (Harper & Row)
- chart paper and markers
- carpet squares

Aim

Children will use creative and expressive-language skills.

Warm-Up

Read aloud *Where the Wild Things Are*, sharing the illustrations. Afterwards, talk about monsters. If necessary, reassure wary fives that there are no such things as the monsters in this book.

Activity

1 Invite children to take an imaginary trip to Monster Mountain, a place where friendly monsters live. Ask, "What do you think Monster Mountain looks like? What do the monsters who live there like to do?" Provide plenty of time for everyone to share ideas.

2 Give each child a carpet square, then ask how the group might use these squares to get to Monster Mountain. Let them use the carpet in whatever imaginative ways they devise.

3 Ask children to find a space on the floor for their carpets. Suggest a chant to start the carpets: "Hands in the air and hands on your nose. Touch the carpet and off it goes! VROOM! WHOOSH!" Invite children to make their own sound effects, or play the music. Ask children what they see along the way and how it feels to fly. When the music stops, guide everyone to a safe landing.

4 Upon returning, invite children to dictate a story about their trip on separate sheets of chart paper, leaving room at the top for children's illustrations. Put the sheets together to create a Big Book about your adventure!

Remember

- Be alert to children's possible fear of monsters. This activity may let them explore their fear.

Observations

- Notice children's ability to create a story through experience rather than props or characterizations.

Books

Rest from your adventure with another monster book.
Boris and the Monsters by Elaine Willoughby (Houghton Mifflin)
Harry and the Terrible Whatzit by Dick Gackenbach (Houghton Mifflin)
How Do You Hide a Monster? by Virginia Kahl (Macmillan)

SPIN-OFFS

- Sing this song to the tune of "The Bear Went Over the Mountain":
  The monster went over the mountain, the monster went over the mountain, the monster went over the mountain, to see what he (she) could see.
  Encourage children to describe what they see on Monster Mountain. Record their ideas in a mountain shape.

Creating a Play
Favorite tales can become new dramas.

Materials

- art and recycled materials for costumes and props
- favorite stories
- flannel-board pieces
- fabric scraps
- sheets

Aim

Children will use creative and expressive-language skills to create their own spontaneous plays.

Warm-Up

Gather children and choose a favorite story together. Fairy tales like *Little Red Riding Hood* or predictable, repetitive books such as *Caps for Sale* (see below) are good choices. Offer many opportunities for children to hear and retell this story. If possible, provide flannel-board pieces so they can experiment with using dialogue in different ways. Children could also write and draw their own versions of the story.

Activity

1 When interest in the story is high, ask children if they would like to experiment with turning it into a play. Invite them to talk about plays they have seen in person, on television, or in the movies.

2 Together, brainstorm things they might need to put on a play, such as costumes, props, and scenery.

Encourage children to examine the art, cloth, and recycled materials around your room and ask, "How can we use these items to make costumes and props for our play?"

3 Talk about where children would like to perform the play. They may want to build a stage in the block area or use the furniture and props in the dramatic-play area.

4 Let children set up for and create their play spontaneously. You can facilitate by providing materials and helping children carry out their ideas.

Remember

- Structured plays with assigned lines are difficult for kindergartners and don't encourage expressive oral language. Those plays are best saved for later years in school.

Observations

Do some children naturally take on the role of director and others of actor? How do they share roles?

Books

These books make good springboards for spontaneous plays.
- *Caps for Sale* by Esphyr Slobodkina (Harper & Row)
- *Let's Make a Play* by Manika Laimgruber (Franklin Watts Inc.)
- *Pardner & Freddie: A Puppet Play* by Courtaney Brooks (Belnice Books)

SPIN-OFFS

- If you have a video recorder, and if children desire, you might try taping their plays. Record them several times so children can see the different versions they create.
- Invite children to write a class storybook version of their play. Children can even write about their playwriting experiences in their journal.

Our Sequenced Story

A book inspires children to tell their own tale.

Materials

- sequenced story
- wooden play person or rag doll

Aim

Children will use creative and expressive-storytelling skills.

Warm-Up

Gather children and read a sequenced story such as *The Very Hungry Caterpillar* by Eric Carle (Putnam Publishing). Ask children to tell what the story is about. Then talk with them about the different parts of the story, including the characters, pictures, and words. Point out that the story has a beginning, a middle, and an end.

Activity

1 Introduce the toy character in an exciting way. Perhaps you could tell children it is shy but has a story to tell. Invite children to help the toy tell its story.

2 Ask children to brainstorm a name for their story's character. Start the story by using the character to set the action. (For example, "Amy is going to school…") Hand off the toy to a child to contribute the next idea for the story. You may find that children incorporate aspects of your warm-up story or other favorite stories as they construct this new tale.

3 Encourage children to continue passing the toy and adding their thoughts to the story until the toy reaches the last child in the circle. Then talk with them about the specific parts of their finished story. Does it have a beginning, middle, and end?

4 Ask children if they would like to make up a new story together. Try using small props such as yarn, toy cars, or other toy people to help children add to their ideas.

Observations

- To what extent do children build on one another's ideas to create the group story? Observe children in their daily activities to see how they build on one another's actions.

Remember

- Children love to create their own roles to dramatize, such as becoming a truck driver, an airplane pilot, a good monster, or a mommy. Help them expand these roles into a greater understanding of the story.

Books

Sequenced stories are fun to follow!
- *Chicka Chicka Boom Boom* by Bill Martin, Jr. (Simon & Schuster)
- *The Little Red Hen* by Lucinda McQueen (Scholastic Inc.)
- *The Snowy Day* by Ezra J. Keats (Viking)

SPIN-OFFS

- Put out art materials, and invite children to draw pictures about their collective story. Use the drawings to make a class book about children's experiences as authors.
- Use sequenced pictures to help children become more familiar with the concepts of beginning, middle, and end. Children can even create their own.

The Little Red Hen

"Not I!" the children may say.

Materials

■ copy of *The Little Red Hen* or another book with a simple, active plot and repetitive phrases

Aim

Children will join in the telling of a familiar story.

In Advance

Become very familiar with the story of the Little Red Hen or another story you choose. It's usually better to learn the characters and the basic sequence of action, rather than trying to memorize the words. Practice telling the story a few times in the mirror or to friends or family.

Warm-Up

Tell a simple story about yourself; for example, something that happened on the way to school. Let children share stories of their own. Explain that people often tell stories instead of reading them.

Activity

1 Gather children and sit comfortably in a large area. If you like, sit in a special "storyteller's chair."

2 Tell children that you are going to tell the story of the Little Red Hen. If children are already familiar with it, talk together about the characters and what happens to them.

3 Tell the story, encouraging children to join in on the repetitive phrase "'Not I', said the cat. 'Not I', said the dog." Signify the end with a concluding phrase such as "And that is the end of our story."

4 Talk about the story together. You might ask children what they liked about it and what they would have done if they were the Little Red Hen or one of the other characters. Also talk about the experience of hearing a story told aloud. How is it different from hearing one read? How is it the same?

Remember

■ Storytelling can be a little intimidating. Remember that you have an appreciative audience who already love to hear any kind of story.

Observations

■ In what ways is children's response to storytelling the same as their response to hearing a story read? In what ways is it different?

Books

These books lend themselves well to storytelling.
■ *Heroes and Heroines, Monsters and Magic* by Joseph Bruchac (The Crossing Press)
■ *Peach Boy and Other Japanese Children's Favorite Stories* by Florence Sakade (Charles Tuttle)

SPIN-OFFS

■ Make felt pieces representing the characters and props in the story. Suggest that children use a felt board to retell the story independently.
■ Bake bread using the ingredients named in the story.

Creature Feature

Creative creatures can inspire a telling tale.

Materials

- children's animal figures from home
- play dough (in a variety of colors)
- small paper plates
- collage items such as toothpicks, buttons, small pebbles, foam pieces, and wallpaper scraps
- glue
- chart paper
- construction paper
- markers

Aim

Children will use creative-thinking and storytelling skills.

In Advance

Ask each child to bring in a stuffed, wooden, or other type of toy animal from home.

Warm-Up

Invite children to talk about and describe their animals. Together, brainstorm different ways they might use this collection of animals in the classroom. Then choose one of their ideas to try. (They might like to make a class zoo or farm, for example.)

Activity

1 Place the animals in an open area, and gather children to discuss their plans. Together, brainstorm a list of other things they would like to create for their project — more animals, food, and so on. Encourage children to talk in pairs or small groups.

2 Put the play dough and other art materials on a table, and invite children to use them to create different creatures and objects.

3 Place the finished creations on a shelf to dry. Create a space for the unfinished items so that children can continue to work on them later.

4 Invite children to talk about their creations. What are they called? What do they eat? How they are used? Ask them to work together to make up and dictate a story about their animals and their creations. Then help children arrange and display their creations along with their written story.

Observations

- What elements of familiar people, places, and things in children's own lives are evident in their creations?

Books

Read these stories for more creative play ideas.
- *Alphabeasts* by Durga Bernhard (Holiday House Inc.)
- *Creatures* by Lee Hopkins (Harcourt Brace & Company)
- *Where the Wild Things Are* by Maurice Sendak (HarperCollins)

SPIN-OFFS

- Invite children to find library books with stories about animals (see Books for ideas). Ask children to compare these stories with their story. They might notice similar animals or settings. Children may find that they can use their own art creations to dramatize the new stories.

Activity Plans
for
Speaking&Listening

Real-life and purposeful opportunities to use oral language skills increase children's potential for academic success.

S trong oral language skills are critical to literacy development because through speaking and listening children first learn how meaning is created and understood. They experience language as a multipurpose tool, one that can be used to inform, to request, to express feeling, and to reflect. When children are at ease with these aspects of oral language use, they can transition to seeing how written language works. They soon recognize the functional importance of a street sign, the pleasure of a picture book, and the personal satisfaction of writing a note or keeping a journal.

Throughout the Day

- Play call-and-response or memory games at group time that encourage children to remember and repeat what they hear.
- Tune in to unique sounds in the environment, and frequently ask children to use descriptive language to tell what they hear.
- Model good listening and speaking skills. Demonstrate this by repeating what you just heard.
- Develop unique sound cues or code words to signal transition times.

Around the Room

- Constantly survey your room for opportunities to plant "conversation starters." Unannounced, you might add a new task to your job chart, put a big umbrella on your class calendar, or put a new name on your attendance chart. Wait and see what children notice, do, or say.
- Set up a "Mystery Box." On a periodic basis, place a mystery object inside a box or a bag. Invite children to reach inside, without looking, to discover what it is. Encourage them to share ideas with one another about how it feels or what it might be.

Last Year, This Year

A new year is meaningful.

Materials

- group photographs from last fall
- photographs of children on special occasions last year, with written descriptions on the back
- sheet of colorful chart paper
- tape
- markers

Aim

Children will examine the concepts of *next* and *last*.

Warm-Up

Explain that in this country, the new year begins in January. Talk about the commonly used "See you next year." What does "next year" mean? What does "last year" mean?

Activity

1 Gather your small group to share the photographs. As you talk together about each photo, emphasize the word *last*. You might say, "This is the picnic we had last fall." "Yvonne, is that the house where you lived last year?" Also, talk with children about their last holiday, last summer, and your last field trip together. Encourage children to refer to the photographs to help them remember.

2 Then ask specific questions to help children compare *next* and *last*. Use children's comments and parents'

written descriptions of photos to help you. For example, you might say, "Becky, you said that at your last birthday party you had a Care Bear on your cake. What do you think you'll want on your next birthday cake?"

3 Record children's responses next to their names on colorful chart paper, being sure to use the words *next* and *last* at the beginning of each statement.

4 Hang the chart on a bulletin board where parents and children can enjoy it together.

Remember

- Children in your group or community may celebrate the new year at different times of year. For example, some may observe the Chinese New Year later in the winter or the Jewish New Year in autumn.

Observations

Note children's use of the words *next* and *last*. What knowledge do they show about the sense of time?

Books

Here are a few wonderful books about changes over time.
- *My Album* by E. Schick (Greenwillow Books)
- *On Mother's Lap* by A. H. Scott (McGraw-Hill)
- *Peter's Chair* by Ezra Jack Keats (HarperCollins)

SPIN-OFFS

- Collect photos taken throughout the year, and ask children to sequence them from left to right by clipping them in a clothesline timeline! Children can share stories with one another about the events in the photos.

When I Was a Baby

It's fun to talk about how we've grown!

Materials

- ethnically diverse baby dolls
- doll furniture such as a high chair, cradle, stroller
- baby items such as a bathing basin, diapers, baby-food jars, baby clothes
- experience-chart paper
- markers

Aim

Children will use thinking, speaking, listening, reading, and writing skills when they compare what they can do now with what they could do when they were babies.

Warm-Up

Set up the dramatic-play area with the baby dolls and baby items, and invite children to play. Observe the activities and discussions that evolve. Ask questions such as "How do you take care of your baby? How does Baby need your help?"

Activity

1 Gather children in front of two sheets of chart paper. Write "Babies can" on one and "I can" on the other. Read the first phrase aloud, and ask children to complete the sentence. Write each child's exact response on the chart paper.

2 Read the phrase "I can," and invite children to take turns completing it. Again, write down each child's exact response. Read the lists together when they are complete.

3 Compare the two charts by rereading the lists, alternating between the two. Tell children you are aware of their increasing abilities: "Wow, look at the things you can do now that you couldn't do as a baby!"

4 Display the charts in an area where children can "read" them on their own and share them with their families.

Remember

- This is a great activity to do when one or more children are expecting or coping with new siblings at home.

Observations

- Notice whether children choose to go back to the charts to read them again. How are they using them?

Books

Share these books about babies at storytime.
- *Bigger Than a Baby* by Harriet Ziefert (HarperCollins)
- *This Little Baby* by Tony Bradman (Putnam Publishing Group)
- *Welcome, Little Baby* by Aliki (Greenwillow Books)

SPIN-OFFS

- Invite parents with babies to visit your class. Ask parents if they'd feel comfortable allowing your children to hold and help change the babies. Then talk to children about what to expect when babies visit your class. Invite the parents to visit regularly so that children can observe the baby's growth and changes (such as size, weight, ability). Keep a *Baby Book* with children's drawings and writings about their observations.

A Magic Pumpkin Journey

Let's take a fantastic pumpkin ride.

Materials

- tape or CD player
- balloons
- gentle instrumental music
- large bag

Aim

Children will use their expressive-language skills and imaginations to create and dramatize an exciting adventure story.

Warm-Up

Gather children in a circle, and invite them to help create and take a pretend journey together. You might ask, "What is an imaginary journey? Have you ever taken one?"

Activity

1 Let children know they will be taking an imaginary journey inside a giant magic pumpkin. Let children's suggestions shape your story as you go along. Ask questions that enable children to decide where the magic pumpkin will go, what makes it move, what dangers will arise, and how those dangers will be overcome. While the magic pumpkin travels, play the instrumental music.

2 At a timely moment, hand out special pumpkins (inflated balloons) to children. Tell them that each of these pumpkins is magical! You might ask, "What kind of magic does your pumpkin have?" or "Where will it go?"

3 Create an ending to the journey by explaining that the magic pumpkins are getting tired. Turn down the volume of the music as you bring out imaginary sleeping bags for children to go to sleep in. Ask children to put the balloons back in the bag, quietly whispering and tiptoeing.

4 Offer children crayons, markers, and paper. Play the same instrumental music you played on your magic pumpkin journey, and invite children to draw pictures and dictate stories about their imagined experiences.

Remember

- Giving time for children to simply observe may help them feel more comfortable about contributing.

Observations

- How are children's individual ideas similar to or different from those in the class story?

Books

Try some other ideas from these movement books.
- *Feeling Strong, Feeling Free* by Molly Sullivan (NAEYC)
- *Kids Make Music* by Avery Hart & Paul Mantell (Williamson)
- *Music and Movement Improvisations* by Miriam B. Stecher (Macmillan)

SPIN-OFFS

- Use children's pictures and stories to create a class book, or audio- or videotape the children telling their stories. Make the book or audiotape a part of your classroom library.

A Creature's Magic Bag

Props inspire creative language.

Materials

- chart paper and markers
- note paper
- large pillowcase
- props such as a hat, big jacket, "magic" stick, pot (kettle), large spoon, rock

Aim

Children will use creative-thinking and language skills as they create a group story.

Warm-Up

Create an imaginary friendly creature with children. Talk about the kinds of things the creature does with its friends and by itself, and where the creature lives. Draw the features of the creature as children suggest them to create a "creature composite." Repeat children's suggestions aloud as you draw to make the connection between their words and your visual clear.

Activity

1 Write the following note and attach it to the pillowcase: "Dear Friends: Here is my magic bag. It is magic because all the things inside tell a magic story. I hope these items help you get to know me. Enjoy! Your Friendly Creature." Show children the pillowcase and read the note.

2 Begin the story by saying "Once upon a time there was a friendly creature…." Continue by using a prop you have pulled from the pillowcase to make up a sentence to add to the story.

3 Then pass the bag to the child next to you. Encourage the child to reach inside the bag, choose an item, and use it to continue the story. Make sure the pillowcase (and story) are passed to each child in the circle until it gets back to you. Then add an ending.

4 Tape-record the story and transcribe it onto paper. Play the recording or read the story to children. Ask them if there is anything they would like to add or change.

Observations

- What kinds of sentences or phrases do children create as they tell their stories?

Books

These books will provide your children with lots of creative language.
- *Confetti: Poems for Children* by Pat Mora (Lee & Low Books)
- *The Man Who Sang the Sillies* by John Ciardi (J. B. Lippincott)
- *Sing a Song of Popcorn* by Beatrice Schenk de Regniers (Scholastic Inc.)

SPIN-OFFS

- Provide children with paper, and ask them to illustrate their sections of the story. Have each child "write" his or her section of the story on the paper as well. Some children may want the teacher to take dictation or transcribe their sections of the story from the tape. As a group, organize the pictures in sequence and bind the pages together to create a book.

How's the Weather?

Let's give a weather report!

Materials

- real or pretend microphone
- tape recorder or video recorder
- chart paper
- markers
- easel
- pointer
- large map (optional)

Aim

Children will make observations and use descriptive and expressive language as they create their own weather reports.

Warm-Up

Ask children what a weather report is and whether they've ever seen one on TV. Suggest that they watch the weather report at home with their families. Talk about why people might need to know the weather in advance. Introduce the word *meteorologist* as someone who studies the weather.

Activity

1 Tell children that they can take turns giving pretend weather reports. Help them think about what they might say. Start by discussing different kinds of weather (snowy, sunny, windy, rainy). Make a list of the different kinds of weather and the things people do in each kind of weather. Ask children what kind of report they would like to give — verbal, visual, or another type.

2 Give children time to prepare, if they wish. For example, they might want to draw weather pictures or think of ways to use the map.

3 Let children give their reports while you record them. Encourage them to use the pointer and easel and to speak into the microphone like real weather forecasters.

4 Invite other children to ask the weather reporter questions about the weather. Then play the tapes back so that children can watch or hear their weather reports.

Remember

Remind children that meteorologists aren't always correct in their predictions, so they don't have to worry about making a mistake.

Observations

- Do some children give factual weather reports? Do some children give reports that are more imaginative or creative?

Books

Share these books about the weather.
- *Cloudy With a Chance of Meatballs* by Judi Barrett (Atheneum Books)
- *Learning About Weather* by Jo E. Moore (Evan Moor Corporation)
- *Mud Puddle* by Robert Munsch (Firefly Books)

SPIN-OFFS

- Set up a weather center for daily reporting and predicting at circle time. Check each day to see if the previous day's prediction was accurate. You might develop an ongoing graph to record weather patterns or the accuracy of your children's predictions.

Beary Special Friends

Stuffed animals are wonderful classroom visitors.

Materials

- stuffed animals
- markers
- chart paper
- camera and film (optional)

Aim

Children will build self-esteem as they share their special stuffed animals.

In Advance

Ask children to bring their favorite teddy bear or stuffed animal to school. Have extras on hand in case some children forget.

Warm-Up

Read a story about stuffed-animal friends, such as *Corduroy* or *Jamaica's Find*.

Activity

1 Invite each child to introduce his or her stuffed animal to the other children. Encourage children to greet all the animal friends who have come to visit their class. Spend a few moments sharing stories about the stuffed animals, such as how long children have had them, whether or not they were gifts, why children like them, and so on.

2 Talk together about how children chose the names for their stuffed animals, and make a list of names on a sheet of chart paper. Read the list together, noting similarities and differences.

3 Encourage children to talk about why their animals are so special and what they like to do with them. Write children's comments next to their animal's names on the chart paper.

4 If possible, take pictures of children with their animals, and place the photos on the chart. Hang the chart where children can reach it and add their own drawings, if they choose.

Observations

- What kinds of stories do children make up about their animals? Do some children use their animals to talk?
- What emotions do children express?

Books

Here are some other stories about precious possessions that you might share with children.

- *The Bag I'm Taking to Grandma's* by Shirley Neitzel (Greenwillow Books)
- *Bear E. Bear* by Susan Straight (Hyperion Books)
- *Gracias, Rosa* by Michelle Markel (Albert Whitman)

SPIN-OFFS

- Invite children to write or dictate stories and to draw pictures or make individual books about adventures with their stuffed-animal friends.
- Put out a variety of jewelry-making materials, such as beads, yarn, and buttons, for children to use to make necklaces, headbands, and other accessories for their animals.

Sock It to Me!

Children and puppets go hand-in-hand.

Materials

- experience-chart paper
- 1 clean sock for each character in the story
- felt or construction-paper scraps
- white glue
- crayons or markers
- scissors
- storybook that children know and like
- tape recorder and audiotape (optional)

Aim

Children will develop and use expressive and creative oral language skills as they use sock puppets to create stories.

Warm-Up

Invite children to choose a favorite book. Look through the pictures to refresh children's memories. You might also want to read the book aloud.

Activity

1 When you feel children are very familiar with the story, invite them to retell it in their own words. Write their version on experience-chart paper and read it aloud. Consider taping it for children to play as often as they wish.

2 Ask children whether they would like to make puppets to act out the story. Sit with them and talk about the puppets they'll need to make. Let each child or group of children choose a character to make.

3 Move to a worktable and offer each child a sock. Help them put one hand in the sock and experiment with opening and closing the mouth. Put out construction paper, felt scraps, markers, glue, crayons, and scissors, and give children time to create their characters.

4 Give children time to play with their puppets. Invite them to use their puppets to retell the story while you tape them. Compare the different stories.

Remember

- Children may sometimes stray from the original plot or story line as they retell the story.

Observations

- Listen for the vocabulary children use in their stories. Do they create dialogue for the puppets or do they talk about the characters?

Books

Here are a few simple favorites children might enjoy acting out.
- *Abuela* by Arthur Dorros (Dutton)
- *Miss Spider's Tea Party* by David Kirk (Scholastic Inc.)
- *Stone Soup* by Marcia Brown (Macmillan)

SPIN-OFFS

- There are several very simple theaters children can make to perform their show: a table theater (turn a table on its side so children can work behind it), a doorway theater (secure a sheet or towel halfway up a doorway — children can sit or kneel behind it), or a window theater. In nice weather, children can stand outside a low, open window and perform for children inside.

Hola Means Hello

Sing a song of greetings.

Materials

■ chart of the word *hello* in different languages.

Aim

Children will listen and speak as they become aware of different places and people.

Warm-Up

Talk about the different ways people in the United States say hello. How are people alike? How are they different? Explain that although people may speak different languages, we all say many of the same things.

Activity

1 Ask, "Why do people say hello?" Encourage children to share a few ways their family and friends greet each other.

2 Explain that together you'll learn how children in other countries, as well as in our own country, say hello. Using the chart, teach children a few ways. For example: Spanish, *hola* (pronounced oh-la); French, *bonjour* (bone-jure); German *guten tag* (goo-ten tog); Hebrew, *shalom* (shah-lome); Chinese, *neehow* (nee-how.) Be sure to include all the languages your children's families speak.

3 Sing this "Hello Song" together, incorporating the different ways to say hello:

Hello, hello. Hello and how are you?
I'm fine. I'm fine.
And I hope that you are too.
Hola, Hola. Hola and how are you?
I'm fine. I'm fine.
And I hope that you are too.

4 Encourage children to say hello in different languages throughout the day. Every few days, greet children in a different language.

Remember

■ Include all the languages spoken by children in your group, but be sensitive to those who are not comfortable "teaching" peers their native language.
■ Check the pictures you share with children for possible hidden stereotypes.

Observations

■ Note children's auditory ability to hear the sounds of foreign words. Can they reproduce them?

Books

These books will also help children learn about other cultures.
■ *Aanni and the Tree Huggers* by Jeannine Atkins (Lee & Low Books)
■ *Abuela* by Arthur Dorros (Dutton)
■ *The Animal Peace Day* by Jan Wahl (Crown)

SPIN-OFFS

■ Learn simple phrases in different languages, such as "good-bye" and "my name is." Encourage children to incorporate their new vocabulary into dramatic-play activities.

If Animals Could Talk

There are many ways to communicate.

Materials

- experience-chart paper
- drawing paper
- crayons
- animal stickers
- scrap craft materials
- stamp pads (optional)
- magazine pictures of animals
- markers
- paste
- rubber animal stamps
- paper bags

Aim

Children will use problem-solving, creative-thinking, and language skills.

Warm-Up

Gather children together, and talk about how animals communicate their needs to us. Ask, "How do you know when a dog is happy? What does a cat do when it wants food?" Make a list of all the ways animals tell us things.

Activity

1 Invite children to think about the animals they might have at home, the pets you have in your setting, and animals they see outside on the playground or in the neighborhood. Together, brainstorm things these animals might say if they could talk.

2 Show a picture of an animal in a funny situation. (Pictures from pet-food ads often show animals with funny expressions or in unlikely situations.) Encourage children to use their imaginations to tell you what that animal might say. Allow time for every child to share ideas.

3 Put out all the magazine pictures, and let each child choose one. Provide art materials so each child can glue his or her picture to a sheet of drawing paper and add drawings to tell the story of what would happen if this animal could talk.

4 Offer to write children's stories, in their exact words, under the pictures. Then, put all the pictures together into a group book titled *If Animals Could Talk*.

Remember

- Some children may have difficulty verbalizing ideas and would rather create pictures to tell the story.

Observations

- Note whether children use dialogue or talk about their picture.

Books

Many books have talking animal characters. Here are a few great ones.
- *Frog and Toad Are Friends* by Arnold Lobel (Scholastic Inc.)
- *Little Bear* by Else Homelund Minarik (Scholastic Inc.)
- *Words About Animals* by David West (Cooper Beach)

SPIN-OFFS

- Put out puppet-making materials, such as craft scraps and small paper bags. Help children make talking animal puppets to use in informal puppet shows. Tape or video-record the show to share with parents.

Going to School

On a bus, on a boat, or in a car pool?

Materials

- experience-chart paper
- drawing paper
- markers and crayons

Aim

Children will practice oral language in a group situation and investigate the relationship between spoken and written words.

Warm-Up

Gather your group and read the book *This Is the Way We Go to School* by Edith Baer (Scholastic) or another good book about the many different ways children get to school. As you read, talk about the different ways people get from one place to another.

Activity

1 Bring an experience chart and a marker to group time. As children watch, label the chart "How we get to kindergarten." Talk about how you get to school. Add details, such as who you say good-bye to, what you eat for breakfast, and what you do when you arrive at school.

2 Invite children to share their stories. Encourage them to talk about who brings them in the morning, where they say good-bye, what that person does next, and what children do next. Talk about riding on a bus or in a car.

Write each child's response next to her name on the experience chart. Use children's exact words to help them understand the relationship of spoken words to print.

3 Offer children drawing paper and crayons or markers. Together, read over the experience chart again, and ask children to create their own pictures about coming to school in the morning.

4 Hang the experience chart where children and families can see it easily. Then help children hang their drawings around the chart.

Remember

- Allow plenty of time for children to respond to your questions.

Observations

- Listen for children's vocabulary in describing events and things. How much detail do they use?

Books

Look in your local library for these books about transportation.

- *Curious George Rides a Bike* by H. A. Rey (Houghton Mifflin)
- *Jamie Goes on an Airplane* by Jill Krementz (Random House)
- *Jason's Bus Ride* by Harriet Ziefert (Viking)

SPIN-OFFS

- Encourage children to brainstorm funny and unusual ways to get to school. Could they ride a dragon or a snail? What if they hopped on one foot? Create a new (and silly) version of *This Is the Way We Go to School* in a song or big book form.

Rhymes and Songs
Language has a rhythm and life of its own.

Materials

- experience-chart paper
- markers and crayons
- children's books based on repetitive chants or rhymes (see suggestions below)

Aim

Children will use expressive-language, receptive-language, and creative-thinking skills.

Activity

1 When you call children to group time, get ready to go outside, or even stir ingredients in a bowl, create a little chant to verbalize the experience. Many children may be inspired to join you or embellish the chant themselves. One chant might be:

Around and around and around we go,
mixing up the batter so.
Around and around and around we go,
mixing up the play dough.

2 Choose a book based on a simple chant, such as *Jesse Bear, What Will You Wear?* by Nanci White Carlstrom (Scholastic). Encourage children to chime in after you've read a few rhymes. Reread the book. This time, leave out the rhyming word at the end of each phrase for children to fill in.

3 Invite them to make up new verses. You might ask, "What else could Jesse Bear wear? What would you add to the chant?" Read the story together many times, inviting children to say more and more of the rhyme each time.

4 Write children's new verses on experience-chart paper, leaving room for them to add illustrations if they'd like. Include the new chants the next time you read the story.

Remember

- When you write children's chants on chart paper, you help them make a connection between the words they say and the words you write.

Observations

- What rhymes particularly appeal to children? What patterns or phrases do they learn more easily?

Books

These books offer wonderful rhymes and chants.
- *If You Give a Mouse a Cookie* by Laura Joffee Numeroff (Scholastic Inc.)
- *Is Your Mama a Llama?* by Deborah Guarino (Scholastic Inc.)
- *See You Later Alligator* by Barbara Strauss and Helen Friedland (Price, Stern, Sloan)

SPIN-OFFS

- Often, song patterns encourage children to make up their own spontaneous chants and rhymes. Use a favorite song to create these add-on chants with your group. If children enjoy "This Old Man," ask, "What else could the old man play on?" Invite children to make up new verses using different items or even new numbers! Then sing each original verse together.

Lots and Lots of Shoes
Familiar objects are often inspiring.

Materials

- variety of shoes, such as ballet shoes, work boots, high heels, sneakers, and silly slippers
- shoe boxes
- note paper
- boxes

Aim

Children will use listening, speaking, reading, writing, gross-motor, and creative-thinking skills.

In Advance

Send a note home to families inviting them to donate old shoes and empty shoe boxes to add to your dress-up collection. If possible, borrow a shoe sizer from a local shoe store.

Warm-Up

Talk about the different types of shoes children are wearing, and encourage them to identify similarities and differences.

Activity

1 Place any newly acquired shoes in the dress-up area. Observe as children try on the shoes and use them as costumes for different roles. At moments when you won't disrupt play, talk about the different pairs of shoes. Encourage children to tell you about who they're pretending to be.

2 Add other props that may inspire new play scenarios, such as shoe boxes and a shoe sizer. Children may want to create a shoe store in the dramatic-play area, with players taking turns being customers and salespeople.

3 Let children take the lead in creating their shoe store, assisting only as needed. Provide paper and markers that children can use to make price tags, write up orders, or give as receipts.

4 Invite shoe store participants to tell about their experience making the store and playing there. They may even have a sale to announce!

Remember

- Be sure that all shoes are clean. It may be necessary to use a spray disinfectant.

Observations

- Do children feel comfortable writing signs and tags in their own way, or do they want you to do it for them instead?

Books

More shoes? Why not!
- *New Blue Shoes* by Eve Rice (Viking Penguin)
- *Shoes* by Elizabeth Winthrop (HarperCollins)
- *What Can You Do With a Shoe?* by Beatrice De Regniers (HarperCollins)

SPIN-OFFS

- Put on some light instrumental music. Ask children to imagine that they are wearing big heavy boots, and encourage them to tell you how they would walk in those boots. Have them try out those movements, then change the imaginary boots to slippers, high heels, a giant's shoes, ice skates, etc. Help children attach descriptive words to their movements, such as *clomping*, *stomping*, *sliding*, and *gliding*.

Animal Observations

Animals can teach us too.

Materials

- heavy cardboard (or other hard surface)
- drawing paper
- colored construction paper
- crayons
- stapler

Aim

Children will use descriptive and analytical language and observation skills as they learn about animals.

In Advance

Scout around your playground or a nearby park for animals or insects children can observe. Plan this activity for one of these areas. Remember: You want to observe but not disturb animal life.

Warm-Up

Prepare children for a walk in the playground or in a nearby park to observe animals and insects. Invite them to be naturalists. You might explain the term this way: "Naturalists are people who study animals. They go on investigations to see what an animal looks like and to watch how it moves, what it eats, and where it lives."

Activity

1 Remind children to be very quiet when you first go outside so they don't frighten away nearby animals. Invite children to look carefully for animals or signs of animals.

2 Encourage them to get down on the ground to look for insects or toads. Invite each child to observe one creature for a while. Remind them to stay in the playground or park. If their animal leaves the area, they can look for another to follow.

3 Ask children to quietly imitate the animals' movements. Beetles are a good choice because they move slowly and are easy to watch. Birds and squirrels are harder to keep up with and more easily frightened.

4 Take time to share observations. Then ask children to draw a picture of the animal or insect they observed. Collate the drawings and observations into a field guide.

Remember

- This is a wonderful activity to do once a week over a period of time so that children get to see how different animals' activities change with the season.

Observations

- Notice the ease or difficulty children experience in describing their observations.

Books

Here are some animal books to share at storytime.
- *Frederick* by Leo Lionni (Random House)
- *The Goodnight Circle* by Carolyn Lesser (Harcourt Brace)
- *A Year of Birds* by Ashley Wolff (Dodd, Mead)

SPIN-OFFS

- Try observing animals in the room, such as hamsters, guinea pigs, and goldfish. Add entries on these animals, or on children's pets at home, to your guide.

The Chit-Chat Corner

Watch conversations flourish.

Materials

- experience-chart paper and markers
- small, quiet, private area of the room (carpeted if possible)
- child-sized furniture, such as pillows, vinyl-covered beanbag chairs, air mattress, or even a big tire tube
- play telephones or disconnected real phones
- toy microphones
- potted plants
- newspapers and magazines
- class pet (if possible)
- puppets
- tape recorder

Aim

Children will build language and social-interaction skills.

In Advance

Find an area in your room that is suitable for quiet play. This should be well away from noisy areas and high-traffic areas such as doorways, cubbies, or sinks. Spread an old piece of carpet or a few area rugs on the floor, and add some comfortable child-sized furniture.

Warm-Up

Open a discussion about the different reasons people talk on the phone: to place pizza orders, to talk to friends, to find out when movies are playing, and so on. Create a list of all the different reasons on an experience chart.

Activity

1 Show children the cozy corner, and talk about ways they might decorate it. Brainstorm a list of additional props, such as walkie-talkies, tape recorder, and message pads.

2 Encourage children to use play telephones, microphones, and other objects that encourage conversation. Children might pretend to talk to stuffed animals, call each other to confirm play dates, or recount exciting trips.

3 To inspire fresh conversation and further language development over time, add new, interesting items such as puppets, plants, or even a small pet to the area.

4 Provide newspapers and magazines, and encourage children to talk over the daily news.

Remember

- Keep an eye on the center, but help children feel free to talk among themselves.

Observations

- How do children resolve conflicts?

Books

Here are some picture books to inspire conversation.
- *Feelings* by Aliki (Greenwillow Books)
- *First Comes Harry* by Taro Gomi (Delmar)
- *Hazel's Amazing Mother* by R. Wells (Dell)

SPIN-OFFS

- Bring in interesting magazines, card games, and checkers to enhance the social conversations in the corner.
- Extend your child-talk philosophy into all areas of your room. Show children you respect their thoughts — bend down to their level when you speak or listen, let them complete their thoughts without interruption, and show interest through your facial and body gestures when a child speaks to you.

Peekaboo, I See a Zoo!

Guessing games build language skills.

Materials

- calendar
- travel and vacation magazines
- scissors
- manila folders
- glue

In Advance

Gather children together to talk about trips and vacations. Encourage them to talk about trips that they or members of their families have taken or would like to take. Record children's ideas on experience-chart paper, and invite them to illustrate the chart.

Activity

1 Move to a table and put out the travel and vacation magazines. Encourage children to look through them and cut or tear out a very large picture of a place where they would like to go or have gone.

2 Give children each a folder, and open it so they can glue their picture to the inside. Then help them cut a two-inch hole through the front cover so that when the folder is closed a small section of the picture inside is visible. You may want to help children look at their picture critically to decide what section they want visible. They may first want to draw the outline of their hole in pencil. They can then cut the cover hole in that spot.

3 Ask children to bring their folders to group time. Invite one child at a time to show his or her closed folder and say something like "I would like to go where there are…" and list some things found at that particular spot. The other children can look at the part of the picture that shows through the hole to guess what place is pictured inside.

4 After taking a number of guesses, each child may open the folder and reveal the full picture. Children can talk about how they decided where to cut the holes in their folders and what guesses they expected others to make. Children can then share further ideas about why they'd like to travel to the places pictured and what they'd like to do there.

Observations

- Look for children's ability to verbalize their destinations and their reasons for going there. Some children may find it easier to choose a place to go than to talk about it.

Books

Share these books about going away.
- *Are We There Yet?* by Margo Mason (Bantam)
- *Mitchell Is Moving* by Marjorie Weinman Sharmat (Scholastic Inc.)
- *Summer Camp* by Bobbie Kalman (Crabtree Publishing)

SPIN-OFFS

- When children leave for trips, offer them a trip log to take along. Staple several sheets of blank paper together and, on the cover, help children write "My Trip to…" Send a note home or talk to parents about ways to help their children keep records of their time away — such as by drawing a picture each day of a special event or experience. Encourage children to share the log when they return.

Activity Plans
for
Letters&Sounds

Children are naturally curious about printed symbols. They will proudly identify letters in their names or on signs. They love to experiment: making a new letter out of one already drawn, turning a letter on its side, or playing a name game. The activities in this section will help you take advantage of "teachable moments" in which children seek to learn more about letters and sounds.

Throughout the Day

- Help children notice the environmental print all around them. They may pick out letters that are in their own names or identify words they have learned to recognize.
- Play with words and sounds when calling children's names or going for a walk. For example, call groups of children whose names begin with the same sound.

Around the Room

- Hang an Alphabet Clothesline (with one clip for each letter) across a corner of your room. Children can clip small items whose names start with a particular letter onto the appropriate clothespin.
- Keep favorite alphabet poems, rhymes, and songs on display. Add new and exciting alphabet books to your library corner. Look for ABC books with a special theme (such as unusual animals) or those that will enhance vocabulary and introduce new concepts.

Environmental print offers children consistent and focused opportunities to explore letters and sounds as well as the functions of written language.

Let's Take a Letter Walk

A neighborhood stroll turns into an alphabet hunt.

Materials

■ index cards   ■ markers   ■ small pad   ■ pencils

Aim

Children will become aware of environmental print outdoors.

In Advance

Print the letters of the alphabet and the numerals from 1 to 10 on individual index cards. Write both uppercase and lowercase letters on the cards. Make extras of letters commonly found on signs in your area.

Warm-Up

Show children the letter and numeral cards, and talk about the letter and numeral names. Ask children to look around the room and point out the letters and numbers they see. Invite children to name letters they know. Note letters that are the initial letters of children's names.

Activity

1 Go outside together and suggest that children widen their search for letters and numbers by looking at signs and buildings. Help children notice that most letters have two different forms (uppercase and lowercase).

2 Give each child a few cards as his or her special letters or numerals to look for. (Be sure that each child has at least one that is relatively easy to find.) Explain that children can help one another find letters and numerals; they don't have to just look for their own.

3 Follow a route that offers many signs, buildings, and vehicles with letters and numerals on them. Encourage children to call out letters and numbers when they see them and to write them on the pad. Occasionally stop and try to figure out the meaning of familiar signs together.

4 Back inside, talk about which letters children seemed to see most often and least often. Keep an alphabet tally sheet. Which letters were found the most?

Observations

■ Are children accustomed to noticing words outdoors, or do they seem to be seeing them for the first time?
■ Note the reading strategies children use to make meaning out of printed signs. Do they note location, size, and purpose? Do they use some knowledge of letters and sounds?

Books

Enjoy these interesting alphabet books before and after your walk.
■ *A, B, See!* by Tana Hoban (Greenwillow Books)
■ *Alfred's Alphabet Walk* by Victoria Chess (Greenwillow Books)
■ *Alphabet World* by Barry Miller (Macmillan)

SPIN-OFFS

■ Make letter rubbings. Take along thin newsprint paper and unwrapped crayons on your walk. Look for signs that have raised letters, and show children how to place the paper over the letters and gently rub the side of the crayon on the paper so the letters or numerals appear.

Create Growth Poems
Introduce personal poetry.

Materials

- chart paper
- markers
- seashells
- crayons
- small bells

Aim

Children will create and illustrate poems about growth.

In Advance

Copy the nursery rhyme "Mary, Mary" (below) onto chart paper.

> *Mary, Mary, quite contrary.*
> *How does your garden grow?*
> *With silver bells and cockleshells,*
> *And pretty maids all in a row.*

Warm-Up

Invite children to say the rhyme together several times. Open a discussion about the words in the rhyme. Suggest that children hold and describe the bells and seashells. Have they ever seen bells and seashells growing in a garden?

Activity

1 Discuss different kinds of growth. Some children might want to describe things they would like to grow in a garden of their own. Others might be more interested in the ways that they themselves are growing. Give the group plenty of time to share their ideas.

2 Invite children to create new versions of the rhyme, featuring their names. Give them time to think.

3 After a few minutes, ask a child to share his or her poem aloud. Variations might sound like:

> *Jesse Smith Jesse Smith/How does your garden grow?/*
> *With shiny cars and tiny trucks/driving by your big toe!* or,
> *Jesse Jesse Jesse Smith/How have you grown this year?/*
> *My foot has grown, my arm has grown/And so has my ear!*

4 Write children's poems on separate sheets of chart paper and let them decorate the pages.

Remember

- Sometimes when children hear rhymes, they feel they have to create them themselves. Assure them that this is not so.

Observations

- Do children like to create factual or more fanciful growth poems?

Books

Here are some good collections of nursery rhymes.
- *A Child's First Book of Poems* illustrated by Cyndy Szekeres (Western Publishing Co.)
- *First Poems of Childhood* illustrated by Tasha Tudor (Putnam)
- *Mother Goose's Nursery Rhymes* illustrated by Allen Atkinson (Alfred A. Knopf)

SPIN-OFFS

- Repeat this activity with other nursery rhymes. Create a class library of personalized poems.
- Make a list of things that grow. Encourage children to add to it and watch your list grow too!
- Invite children to create their own garden landscapes modeled after their versions of the rhyme. Provide a variety of natural and human-made materials.

Rhythm and Rhyme

Poems inspire our bodies and our minds.

Materials

- books of rhymes or poems
- experience-chart paper
- instrumental music
- marker
- tape player
- handkerchief or scarf for each child (optional)

Aim

Children will use movement to experience the rhythm and express the rhymes of a poem.

In Advance

Choose a poem and write it on chart paper. Invite a few children to help illustrate it.

Warm-Up

Read or recite the poem aloud. Be expressive so that children can begin to feel the movement and rhythm of the verse. Move your hands, shoulders, or head to the beat of the words as you read. Encourage children to do the same as they listen carefully to the rhythmic language.

Activity

1 Clear a space in the classroom, and put on instrumental music that suits the mood of the poem. Give children a few moments to move freely. Then lower the volume, and read the poem aloud as the music plays softly in the background.

2 Encourage children to move freely to the music and words of the poem as you read. Offer the handkerchiefs or scarves, if available.

3 Sit down in a circle and bring out your chart. Read the poem slowly, pointing to the words and emphasizing the rhythm and the rhymes. Ask children what they notice about the sounds and letters of the rhyming words, and talk about their comments.

4 Suggest that children invent their own special movements to indicate rhyming words. Put the music back on and read the poem again. Invite children to perform their special movements when they hear words that rhyme.

Observations

- Do children recognize rhyming sounds? Are they able to express their understanding of rhyme through movement?

Books

Here are a few good poetry and rhyme books to share with children.
- *The Dog Laughed* by Lucy Cousins (E. P. Dutton)
- *Gorilla! Chinchilla* by Bert Kitchen (Puffin Books)
- *Still as a Star* by Lee Bennett Hopkins (Little, Brown)

SPIN-OFFS

- Young children often create rhymes spontaneously while playing. Write a few down exactly as children say them, even if the rhymes are nonsense. Share them again at group time.
- Create classroom rhymes to indicate times of transition between activities. Collect and write down these rhymes in a class book.

Follow the Leader

Listen and create.

Materials

- two-sided easel
- drawing paper
- paintbrushes
- tempera paint

Aim

Children will use their listening and speaking skills as they share an art experience.

Warm-Up

Play a listening game. Ask children to close their eyes while you make familiar sounds such as clapping hands, pouring water, tearing paper, or ringing a bell. Invite children to try identifying these different sounds. Then ask children to take turns creating other sounds for their classmates to identify. Some possibilities are shaking a rattle, crumpling newspaper, banging blocks, and sharpening a pencil.

Activity

1 Ask two children to stand on opposite sides of the easel. Choose one to be the leader and the other to be the follower. Explain that the roles will be reversed later in the activity.

2 Tell the leader to slowly paint lines and shapes on his or her sheet of paper. At the same time, the leader should give instructions that the follower can use to copy the designs onto his or her own paper. The leader might say, "I'm painting a long blue line on the bottom of the paper. Now I'm making a large red dot in the middle of the paper."

3 When both have finished painting the designs, have the two children compare their pictures. Ask open-ended questions like " How are your paintings the same? How are they different?" Invite the follower to share what helpful directions the leader gave.

4 Put new sheets of paper on opposite sides of the easel and repeat the activity, with children switching the roles of leader and follower.

Observations

- Notice how children interpret the verbal instructions they hear from their classmates.

Books

Here are some special listening books:
- *A Fly Went By* by Mike McClintock (Random House)
- *A Kiss for Little Bear* by Else Homelund Minarik (HarperCollins)
- *The Happy Owls* by Piatti (Atheneum)

SPIN-OFFS

- Divide children into pairs. Ask one child to tap a rhythm on the drum while the other child listens. The listening child then tries to clap the drum's rhythm. Encourage drumming children to make clear, simple rhythms.
- Invite two children to sit back to back, each with 20 or more blocks. Have one child build a structure and describe it to the other child to build. Then reverse roles.

Baking Banana Bread

Learning is most fun when it's tasty!

Materials

- a 9" x 5" baking pan
- measuring cups and spoons
- chart paper
- markers
- bowls
- wooden spoon

Aim

Children will have fun exploring the letter *b* while baking.

In Advance

Write a recipe for banana bread on chart paper. (Use the one here or your own favorite.) Make the *b*'s a different color to highlight them.

Warm-Up

Talk about banana bread and about baking. Read over your recipe chart together. Be sure children understand all the terms, and point out the *b* words as you go.

Activity

1 Preheat the oven to 350°. After children wash their hands, help them with the following steps. Refer to the recipe chart often, and note the *b* words you find.

2 Grease the loaf pan, and mash three small bananas to make one cup. Measure out the following ingredients: 1 cup each whole wheat and white flour, 1 teaspoon baking

soda, $\frac{1}{2}$ teaspoon each baking powder and cinnamon, $\frac{1}{4}$ teaspoon nutmeg. Take turns mixing them in a bowl.

3 In another bowl, beat together $\frac{1}{2}$ cup vegetable oil and $\frac{1}{2}$ cup honey, until smooth. Beat in 2 eggs, 1 teaspoon vanilla extract, and the bananas, and mix well. Then combine the wet and dry mixtures and pour into the loaf pan.

4 Bake until done, about 60 to 70 minutes. Cool for at least two hours before slicing.

Remember

- Cooking together involves math and science learning as well as language. Point out measurements, changes in appearance, and other interesting aspects of the cooking process.

Observations

- Which aspects of the activity do children find most interesting? Are they excited about finding *b* words?

Books

Try these titles for other letter learning.
- *Brown Bear, Brown Bear, What Do You See?* by Bill Martin, Jr. (Henry Holt)
- *Good Night Gorilla* by Peggy Rathman (Putnam Pub. Group)
- *Pumpkin, Pumpkin* by Jeanne Titherington (Greenwillow)

SPIN-OFFS

- Make an alphabet cookbook with recipes for favorites such as apple pie and carrot cake. Ask families to donate recipes.
- Invite children to create recipes for their favorite foods. Have children write and illustrate recipe cards for a class recipe file box.

The Rhyming Board

Change one letter, make a new word!

Materials

- cardboard, about 3" x 8"
- Velcro tape
- index cards
- markers

Aim

Children will practice rhyming and word patterns.

In Advance

Position two pieces of Velcro on the cardboard so that two index cards can be attached side by side. Attach the opposite portion of the Velcro to 10 cards.

Warm-Up

Have fun reading a rhyming book with children. Do this several times so children become familiar with it.

Activity

1 Bring chart paper and the prepared materials to group time. Read the story again, then write down a rhyming word from it, such as *boom* from *Chicka Chicka Boom Boom*. Read the word slowly, pointing to the letters. Together, brainstorm other words (including nonsense words) that have the *oom* sound. Write down children's ideas.

2 Write the letter *b* on one index card and the rhyme pattern *oom* on another, then attach them to the rhyming board. Show children how they combine to make the word *boom*. Together, think of a rebus for *boom* and draw it on the *b* card to help children remember the word and sound.

3 Ask children to choose another rhyming word from the chart, perhaps *zoom*. Write a *z* on another index card, and invite a child to replace the *b* with the *z*. Again, draw a rebus. Talk about how you created a new word by just changing one letter. Repeat this a few times to make several words.

4 Set out the book, list of words, rhyming board, index cards, and markers in your reading center. Encourage children to use the cards or to create new rhyming words.

Observations

- Do children seem to understand how to use the rhyming board independently, or do they need more practice as a group?

Books

These books are great for rhyming.
- *Chicka Chicka Boom Boom* by Bill Martin, Jr. (Simon & Schuster)
- *Is Your Mama a Llama?* by Deborah Guarino (Scholastic Inc.)
- *Where's My Teddy?* by Jez Alborough (Candlewick)

SPIN-OFFS

- Write simple words on index cards and add rebuses. Let children arrange the cards to make short, simple stories.
- Choose a familiar poem such as "One, Two, Buckle My Shoe," and encourage children to substitute words that will fit the same rhythmic pattern.

Nursery Rhyme Time

Make your own big book of rhymes.

Materials

- chart paper
- markers and crayons
- binder rings
- clear self-adhesive paper

Aim

Children will use nursery rhymes to practice rhyming sounds.

Warm-Up

Bring in a book of nursery rhymes. Read a few aloud, then discuss the rhymes with the group. Have children heard them before? Do they have other favorite rhymes? Can they remember and recite any nursery rhymes?

Activity

1 Choose one nursery rhyme to start with and write it out, line by line, on chart paper. (You can do this outside of class time or as children watch.) At group time, read the rhyme aloud several times. Emphasize sounds on the first one or two readings, then point out letter patterns as well.

2 Invite a small group of children to illustrate the rhyme on the chart paper. When children finish decorating the nursery rhyme, laminate the chart paper or cover it with clear self-adhesive paper.

3 Repeat this process with three or four other nursery rhymes over the next few days. Punch holes along the sides of each one after children have illustrated it. Combine the rhymes, attached with binder rings, to make a class book for all to enjoy.

4 Read the nursery rhymes periodically, and leave them out for children to read independently. Use the nursery rhymes repeatedly over time to help you talk about rhyming words, initial consonants, and other language learning.

Remember

- Poems, songs, and chants are also good sources for rhyming. Select a variety of literature with a strong emphasis on rhymes, patterned language, and word play. Look for examples that represent your children's cultures.

Observations

- Are some children able to chime in on rhyming words? Do they recite the nursery rhymes from memory?

Books

These nursery-rhyme collections stand out from the crowd.
- *Babushka's Mother Goose* by Patricia Polacco (Philomel)
- *Mother Goose's Words of Wit and Wisdom* by Tedd Arnold (Dial)
- *Tomie dePaola's Mother Goose* (G. P. Putnam's Sons)

SPIN-OFFS

- Sit in a circle and recite "Humpty Dumpty." Ask each child to make up a rhyme for his or her name, such as "Thomas Pomas." Clap out a rhythm and have children take turns calling out their name rhymes.
- Choose a common rhyming pattern, such as *all*. Brainstorm words that rhyme with it, then go on a "rhyming treasure hunt" by looking for the items around your room.

Boxes Full of Words

Certain words are important.

Materials

- index cards
- permanent marker
- index card box for each child
- crayons or markers

Aim

Children will become familiar with words and letter-sound relationships, using words they choose themselves.

In Advance

Choose a few words that are meaningful to you personally, such as the names of people in your family, your favorite food, or something you enjoy doing. Write them on index cards, and store them in an index-card box.

Ask families to send in a list of the names of family members, pets, and special friends so you will know the correct spellings.

Warm-Up

Show children your index cards and box, and read the words. Talk about why these words are important to you and ways you might use them when reading or writing.

Activity

1 Meet one-on-one with each child. Offer an index card box, and ask the child to write his or her name on the box with the permanent marker, helping out if needed. Then ask the child to name a few things that are important to him or her. Write the words on the cards, saying them aloud as you write.

2 Read each word slowly a few times. Ask children what they notice about the letters in the words. Talk about the letters — what the first and last letters are and whether any letters repeat.

3 Suggest that children draw a picture on the back of each card to help them remember what the word is. Offer crayons or markers.

4 Encourage children to use their words to write their own letters, stories, or signs. Help them add new words to their boxes periodically.

Observations

- Do children show feelings of excitement and pride at having their "own" words?

Books

These books are written by children for children.
- *Oliver and the Oil Spill* by Aruna Chandrasekhar (Landmark Editions, Inc.)
- *Patulous the Prairie Rattlesnake* by Jonathan Kahn (Landmark Editions, Inc.)
- *Who Can Fix It?* by Leslie Ann Mackeon (Landmark Editions, Inc.)

SPIN-OFFS

- Word boxes and journal writing are perfect partners. If possible, set aside time every week for children to write or draw in their journals about any topic that interests them.
- At group time, write a large letter on chart paper. Ask children to look through their word cards and find words that start with that letter.

"P-Art" Projects

"Pass the paper, please!"

Materials

- construction paper
- paper scraps
- paints and brushes
- pencils
- chart paper and marker
- scissors
- old magazines
- glue

Aim

Children will become familiar with the sound of the letter *p* through an art activity.

In Advance

Ask a few children to help you tear scraps of tissue, construction, and other types of paper to use as collage materials. Ask other children to look through magazines and cut out pictures of objects that start with *p*.

Warm-Up

Talk about the letter *p*. Ask children to name words that start with that sound. Record them on chart paper.

Activity

1 Turn to your art center, and together, brainstorm all the things there that start with *p*.

2 Encourage children to help you organize your art center as a "P-art" center, featuring all the materials they found that start with the letter *p*.

3 Offer each child a large sheet of construction paper, and invite everyone to paint, draw with pencils, or paste materials to create individual art projects. Encourage children to talk to each other as they create and have fun pointing out the *p* words they use.

4 As children work, listen to their comments and write down some of their *p* words and phrases. Later, copy the words onto separate strips of construction paper or in any way that makes them attractive and readable. Display the words in your classroom along with children's art creations.

Remember

- Continue to add more *p* materials to the chart, especially those suggested by children.

Observations

- Do children stick to one form of art (drawing, painting, or collage), or do they readily combine the forms? What combinations do they make?

Books

Look for these unusual alphabet books.
- *Alphabeasts: A Hide and Seek Alphabet Book* by Durga Bernhard (Holiday)
- *Anno's Alphabet: An Adventure in Imagination* by Anno Mitsumasa (Harper)
- *A Farmer's Alphabet* by Mary Azarian (Godine)

SPIN-OFFS

- Make "p soup" using stock, dried peas, chopped parsley, and small pasta. (Look especially for acini pepe to fit the theme.)
- Encourage children to incorporate the *p* sound throughout the day. Invite them to say new versions of each other's names by beginning with the *p* sound — for example, Pavid or Pusan.

Activity Plans
for
Writing

Children's own writing offers the best insight into their understanding of print, including their letter/sound knowledge. These activities will inspire children to explore expressing their ideas on paper, while helping you build a collection of children's work. Over time, you will be able to document — for yourself, parents, and children themselves — the ways in which children experiment with language to learn how it works.

Children's ongoing writing explorations often provide strong insight on reading development, including the understanding of phonetic principles.

Throughout the Day

- Ask children to write their names on a sign-in sheet when they arrive in the morning.
- Write a morning and an afternoon message to children each day to model different forms of writing.
- Encourage children to draw, paste, or write in their own notebooks or journals every day.

Around the Room

- Create a writing center stocked with a variety of writing implements and papers that inspire children to draw and write.
- Add pads and paper to other learning centers. Children can take phone messages and write shopping lists in the dramatic-play corner while others are writing dimensions and building specs in the block area. Put paper and crayons by the fish tank or near a window for children to record nature observations.
- Create a word wall of children's favorite and most-used words. Add an illustration next to each word so children can use it as a picture dictionary.

Make a Letter Book

Favorite letters can inspire a book.

Materials

- markers
- pencils
- watercolors
- old magazines
- crayons
- drawing paper
- scissors
- paste

Aim

Children will explore the alphabet and then create letter books.

In Advance

Using white drawing paper, make blank books.

Warm-Up

Display an alphabet chart or alphabet letter cards. Ask children to identify the letters and brainstorm a word that begins with each letter. An easy place to begin is with the letter that begins each child's name.

Activity

1 Invite children to choose their favorite letter and use it to illustrate the cover of the blank book. Children might consult favorite alphabet books for illustration ideas. Encourage them to share their ideas with one another, especially if several children find they have chosen the same letter.

2 Take out crayons, pencils, markers, watercolors, old magazines, and scissors. Have each child either illustrate or cut out and paste magazine pictures of objects whose names begin with their chosen letter.

3 Have children caption their pictures with either the letter or the word identifying the object.

4 Encourage children to share books with each other. Invite children to continue adding new pictures to their books as they learn new words that begin with that letter. Children may even decide to begin new books that feature other letters.

Observations

- When children trade their letter books, are they able to identify the letters and words through other children's interpretations?

Books

Here are some interesting alphabet books for children to examine.
- *Frog Alphabet Book* by Jerry Pallotta (Charlesbridge)
- *Guinea Pig ABC* by Kate Duke (Dutton)
- *26 Letters and 99 Cents* by Tana Hoban (Scholastic Inc.)

SPIN-OFFS

- Invite children to construct an alphabet city out of wooden blocks. They might build three-dimensional structures that represent the letters of the alphabet.
- They can fill their city with objects and drawings whose names begin with the corresponding letters.

What Will I Call It?

Create your own title.

Materials

- photographs of famous abstract artwork
- construction-paper scraps
- magazines
- postcards
- cards
- markers
- tempera paints
- watercolors
- paper
- crayons
- marbles

Aim

Children will use observation, creative language, and writing skills.

In Advance

Collect samples of famous abstract art from library books, old calendars, and postcards. Look for simple abstracts, such as the work of Pollack, Miró, Picasso, and Klee.

Warm-Up

Talk about paintings and why people create them. Do pictures always have to look a certain way?

Activity

1 Show children a picture of an abstract painting. Explain that many artists give their pictures names, or titles. Ask children to guess the title of the picture you are looking at. Different children will see different things in the picture. Encourage them to use their imaginations to entitle the pictures.

2 After you've listed all the suggestions and maybe one or two of your own, tell children what the title really is and include it on your list. (This activity works best if you choose a very abstract painting that has an unusual name.)

3 Share other pictures and titles, helping children notice that the title may have something to do with how the picture looks.

4 Provide art materials for children to create their own works of art. Try dipping marbles in paint and rolling them on paper.

Remember

- There is no right or wrong name for these pictures. Invite children to come up with creative titles!

Observations

- What information do children use to create their titles? Do they relate to the artwork?

Books

- *Ernie's Work of Art* by Valjean McLenighan (Western Pub.)
- *Jackson Makes His Move* by Andrew Glass (Frederick Warne)
- *Life Doesn't Frighten Me at All* by Maya Angelou (Henry Holt)
- *Marc Chagall, Artstart Very First Art Books* by Ernest Raboff (HarperCollins)

SPIN-OFFS

- Place colored geometric shapes on a large sheet of paper for a collage effect. Encourage children to use watercolors and a brush to make a painting out of many dots. As children finish, ask them to study their paintings and title them. Provide file cards so they can write their titles with inventive spelling (or you can take dictation). Display the masterpieces on a special bulletin board with titles attached.

The Kindergarten Times
A story is breaking!

Materials

- newspaper (*USA Today*, for example)
- chart paper
- white paper
- crayons
- markers

Aim

Children will listen, speak, read, and write as they create a newspaper.

Warm-Up

Show children the newspaper. Ask, "Why do people read newspapers?" Invite children to share their ideas and experiences. Identify sections such as the comics, sports, puzzles, and weather forecast.

Activity

1 Tell children that together they will create their own class newspaper. Post a blank sheet of chart paper, and explain that you'll use one sheet for each section. You might start with a page titled "Weather."

2 Record children's words as they share reports of the current weather. Then ask them to predict tomorrow's weather. Let them illustrate the page.

3 Invite a familiar person, such as the custodian, to be interviewed for the paper. Before your guest arrives, ask children to suggest questions they'd like to ask about the person's job, family, or favorite activities. Write the questions on chart paper. As children interview the visitor, sum up each response below the question.

4 Create and illustrate pages on projects, field trips, news from home, and so on. Decide together on a name for the newspaper, and add it to the library corner.

Remember

- Kindergartners enjoy long-term projects. Some children may want to set up a newspaper office in your theme center. Stock it with paper, markers, a typewriter, stamps and stamp pads, and a telephone.

Observations

- How well do children understand the nonfictional quality of news reporting?
- Do children relate newspapers to other important print tools like magazines and recipes?

Books

Try these books for information about reporting the news.
- *Little Store on the Corner* by Alice P. Miller (Scholastic Inc.)
- *Too Hot in Potzburg* by Seymour Fleishman (Albert Whitman)
- *What Can She Be? A Newscaster* by Gloria Goldreic (Lothrop, Lee & Shepard)

SPIN-OFFS

- Plan a field trip to a real newspaper office before or after you create your class newspaper.
- Create a "Daily News" chart. At group time, ask children to dictate news they wish to share about themselves or their families as you record it on chart paper. Throughout the day, encourage children to share bulletins. Challenge children to talk about current events.

Create a Calendar

What's happening this month?

Materials

- experience-chart paper
- scissors
- crayons or markers
- calendar
- collage materials
- masking tape
- large sheet of mural paper
- pencils
- glue and glue brushes
- construction paper

Aim

Children will write, problem-solve, and cooperate to design a calendar of important events.

Warm-Up

Open a discussion about events children are looking forward to, such as birthdays, trips, holiday celebrations, or relatives coming to visit. Write children's comments on an experience chart. Present the calendar, and talk about why and how people use calendars. Discuss a calendar's various components. Suggest that children work together to make a calendar to keep track of their special events.

Activity

1 Ask children for their ideas about making the calendar. How do they think it should look? What materials will they need? Record their ideas and gather the materials.

2 Make an outline of a calendar on a large sheet of mural paper. Encourage children to fill in the numbers.

3 Invite each child to choose a special event to represent on the calendar. Help children find the appropriate boxes in which to record their events. (In some cases, children might want to learn the correct dates from their families and fill in their boxes later.)

4 Encourage children to use collage materials to represent their special events. If they choose, help them write the names of the events as well. Hang the calendar near your group area. At a large-group meeting, invite children to talk about their calendar with the rest of the group.

Remember

- Be sure each child has a personally meaningful event to represent on the calendar. You might want to make a calendar representing several months to make sure everyone is included.

Observations

- How do children explain the function of a calendar? What information are they able to notice on the calendar?

Books

Here are some books about get-togethers.
- *Always Room for One More* by Sorche Nic Leodhas (Henry Holt)
- *Knock! Knock!* by Jackie Carter (Scholastic Inc.)
- *The Relatives Came* by Cynthia Rylanta (Bradbury)

SPIN-OFFS

- Invite children to bring in calendars from home. Talk about ways that the calendars are the same and different. Display the collection in your group time area.

Celebrations Chain
Let's link everyone's customs.

Materials

- construction paper strips in a variety of colors
- glue   ■ stapler
- clothespins

Aim

Children will learn about similarities and differences among family rituals.

In Advance

Send home a note explaining this activity and its purpose, describing how you would like families to participate.

Warm-Up

Invite children to share memories of special times with their families. What are their favorite holidays?

Activity

1 Give each child five paper strips to take home. Explain that you'd like children to talk with their families about holidays and choose favorite things together to write down on the strips. Ask them to be specific, for example: "Visit Aunt Sandra and Uncle Dean in Virginia," or "Eat cookies and potato pancakes."

2 The next day, gather the group and invite children to talk about what they've written on their strips.

3 Point out similarities, such as visiting family or eating special foods. If some children do very different things, such as going on vacation or not celebrating at all, make clear that their customs are also valued.

4 Help children turn their strips into links by stapling or gluing the ends together to make a paper chain. When everyone's strips have been joined, use clothespins to hang the chain as a decoration in your room.

Remember

- Use colors that are symbolic of the holidays everyone in your class celebrates.

Observations

- How well are children able to explain unfamiliar words and ideas related to their holidays? How do other children respond? (You can help by learning ahead of time about how your children celebrate.)

Books

These stories show three very different ways of celebrating the same holiday.
- *Christmas Tree Memories* by Aliki (HarperCollins)
- *Everett Anderson's Christmas Coming* by Lucille Clifton (Henry Holt)
- *Too Many Tamales* by Gary Soto (G. P. Putnam's Sons)

SPIN-OFFS

- Invite a few people from your school or community who celebrate holidays not represented in your classroom. Ask your guests to make paper links about their holidays, and add them to your chain.
- Let each child write and draw a page about his or her celebrations. Combine the pages into a book called *How We Celebrate.*

Look What I Can Do!

Boost self-esteem and encourage reading and writing too.

Materials

- 1 coffee can or shoe box for each child
- experience-chart paper
- markers
- 4" x 8" cards or papers
- crayons
- primary pencils
- scissors
- magazines
- glue

Aim

Children will use creative-thinking, speaking, drawing, and writing skills.

Warm-Up

Ask children to each tell about something they can do that they feel proud of. As children offer ideas, make an "I Can" experience chart by writing their names and their selected accomplishments. (Some children might want to write their own names, especially if doing so is an accomplishment they are proud of!) When the list is complete, read it back together. Leave the chart up so that children can add illustrations if they choose.

Activity

1 Set out markers or crayons, magazine, scissors, and glue on a low table. Offer everyone a card. Ask children to use these materials to illustrate themselves doing something they are proud of.

2 When they finish, they can write their "I can" statements on the back of the cards. Encourage children to use invented spelling or to copy words from the chart.

3 Provide additional cards for children who want to illustrate more than one accomplishment.

4 Invite children to paste their cards onto their can. Talk about uses for their "I Can" cans, such as storage.

Remember

- Children will have very different accomplishments. Be sure all children feel supported in whatever they choose to celebrate, no matter how small.
- Share in one another's accomplishments. Encourage children to talk about the contents of their cans at group time, or with friends during free-play times.

Observations

- Do children have difficulty choosing an accomplishment? What writing techniques do children use to record their accomplishments?

Books

Try these books to continue discussions.
- *I Can Do It Myself* by Lessie Little and Eloise Greenfield (Thomas Y. Crowell)
- *Leo the Late Bloomer* by Robert Krauss (E. P. Dutton)
- *Look What I Can Do* by Jose Aruego (Macmillan)

SPIN-OFFS

- Throughout the year, invite children to document their accomplishments by adding cards to their "I Can" cans. Let them know that an accomplishment is anything they feel proud of, such as learning to tie their shoes, reaching the top of the climber, making a new friend, counting to 100, or anything else they want it to be.

What's in the Mail?
Children love writing letters.

Materials

- props such as old envelopes, junk mail, stickers, stamps and stamp pads
- individual mailboxes (see ideas below)
- crayons
- hollow or unit blocks
- tape
- large cloth bag
- large box

Aim

Children will use drawing and writing skills.

In Advance

Create individual mailboxes for play. You might give each child a sheet of paper to decorate. Then, together, cover clean, large-sized juice cans. Help children label them with their name or special sign or sticker. Or give each child a whole paper plate and half of another. Together, staple the half plate wrong-side-out onto the whole plate to create a pocket. Let children decorate and label.

Warm-Up

At group time, ask children what they think happens when a letter is mailed and what they think goes on at a post office. Elicit children's ideas for how to set up and play a post-office game in the block area. Display and discuss the post office props. Talk about the kinds of messages children might want to send to one another.

Activity

1 Encourage children to create a post office with blocks. After the post office is built, help children choose the job they wish to do. Some possibilities are selling stamps, fastening stamps to letters, rubber-stamping letters, and delivering mail.

2 Invite children to write messages or draw pictures for their classmates and bring them to the post office.

3 Show children other post office props you've collected. Give them plenty of time to play and develop themes. You might be a customer and ask, "Where do I buy stamps? Where can I mail letters?"

4 After the letters are sent and processed, mail carriers can deliver them to children's mailboxes or cubbies.

Observations

- Which children are interested in sending letters to their classmates? What kinds of mail do they send?

Books

Share these books about the post office.
- *I Write It* by Ruth Krauss (Harper & Row)
- *Messages in the Mailbox: How to Write a Letter* by Loreen Leedy (R. R. Bowker)
- *A Visit to the Post Office* by Sandra Ziegler (Children's Press)

SPIN-OFFS

- Try acting out this silly poem with your children.

Mail Myself to You (based on a poem by Woody Guthrie)
I'm gonna wrap myself in paper, I'm gonna dab myself with glue —
Stick some stamps on top of my head, I'm gonna mail myself to you!

Creating a Journal
Try the joys of journal writing.

Materials

- black-and-white speckled notebooks with unlined paper or small books made with unlined white paper
- stapled construction paper cover
- ring binders with hole-punched plain and color paper and/or scrapbook-style books
- pencil
- crayons

Aim

Children will use expressive-language and expository skills.

Warm-Up

Introduce the concept of journal writing by sharing some of your own journal, diary, or personal scrapbook. Note that a journal is a place to write about things that have happened. Talk with children about reasons for keeping a journal and suggest that they each begin one of their own.

Activity

1 Set aside a "writing workshop" time at the beginning of the day during which everyone takes out his or her journal and draws or writes. Children might like to talk about events from home or new experiences and skills.

2 Circle the room as children work in their journals. Offer help and encouragement as children write.

3 Throughout the day, encourage children to write in their journals during free play or whenever they have a thought they would like to record.

4 Provide a sharing time for children to show and "read" what they have written.

Remember

- Some children will start out by drawing a picture and perhaps adding a word or label for it. Others will write a few letters they know. Eventually, children will start writing strings of letters and even phrases and sentences.

Observations

- How do children feel about writing in their journals? Do they have much to say or do they have difficulty getting started?

Books

Use these books for ideas about writing with children.
- *The Art of Teaching Writing* by Lucy McCormick Callkins (Heinemann)
- *On the Road to Literacy* by Ellen Booth Church (Creative Edge)
- *What Did I Write?* by Marie Clay (Heinemann)

SPIN-OFFS

- Write class journals: a trip journal, a vacation journal, a nature-observation journal.
- Choose a story to read to the class in which the main character experiences a very happy or sad event. Invite children to write a journal entry as if they were the character in the story. Have children share their entries.

Our Own Word Book

We can make a dictionary.

Materials

- children's word books and picture dictionaries
- drawing paper
- glue
- scissors
- stapler
- pencils
- old magazines

Aim

Children will select pictures for a class word book.

Warm-Up

Let children look through the word books and picture dictionaries. Ask them to talk about what kinds of books they think these are and how the books might work. Help children discover that the books pair written words with pictures that show what the words mean.

Activity

1 Help children team up into pairs. Look again at the books you have, and notice how the pages show different categories or themes, such as "at the farm" or "in the park." Help each pair of children choose a theme to work on for the class word book.

2 Provide scissors and old magazines, and let children cut out pictures to fit their themes. Encourage children to talk about their choices, and decide together which pictures to select.

3 Next offer drawing paper, glue, and pencils, and ask children to arrange their pictures to create a page. Encourage them to use invented spelling to write their theme across the top and to label each picture.

4 When all the pairs are finished, staple the pages together to create a class word book. Over time, encourage children to add new pictures and pages.

Remember

- Discussing and even arguing with their partners allows children to practice important thinking and language skills. Try not to step in unless children are at an impasse or a discussion becomes heated.

Observations

- How does each pair of children work together to choose pictures and spell words?

Books

Look for these super word books to help increase children's vocabularies.
- *One Hundred Words About Animals* by Richard Brown (Harcourt Brace Jovanovich)
- *One Hundred Words About Transportation* by Richard Brown (Harcourt Brace Jovanovich)
- *Richard Scary's Biggest Word Book Ever!* by Richard Scary (Random House)

SPIN-OFFS

- As a group, create an imaginary place. Ask children to each draw a creature or object they imagine would be found there and then make up a name for it and write it, using invented spelling. Hang the creations in the classroom.
- Challenge children to point out unfamiliar words they see or hear. Keep a running list of these words, defining them as you go.

Activity Plans
for
Making Books

Children are purposeful and creative in learning written language. They will show interest in writing they can really use, like letters to friends or lists of things to do. However, you are likely to find that writing a story is often their favorite way to express themselves. Helping children direct their creative story energy into making a book can be a challenging but personally rewarding experience for them. The activities in this section offer both collaborative and individual bookmaking opportunities.

Throughout the Day

- Anytime is a good time for storytime. The more experiences children have listening to, sharing, and exploring books, the greater the likelihood of future success in reading and writing.
- Create an author/illustrator center. Invite children to choose a favorite author to study. Collect, read, and compare the author's books, and invite children to create their own book in the style of the author/illustrator.
- Display related child-made and class-made books in all learning centers for children to read independently.

Around the Room

- In the writing center, set out blank books in a variety of sizes and shapes for children. Provide loose paper, crayons, and staplers, and imaginations may fly.
- Create a special bookcase or shelf to display children's individual and class books. Set aside time for silent reading in this book area.
- Establish an author's chair as a place for children to read and celebrate their books at group time.

Children feel a unique and special pride when they realize they can be authors and illustrators.

How Is a Book Made?

Many parts make up this process.

Materials

- 9" x 12" sheets of cardboard
- embroidery needles with large eyes
- heavy thread
- scissors
- 8½" x 11" sheets of white paper
- 10" x 14" sheets of wallpaper or wrapping paper
- glue

Aim

Children will learn about the structure of books by making their own.

In Advance

Cut the cardboard sheets in half. To prepare for sewing, double-thread needles with one foot of thread, and tie both ends into large knots.

Warm-Up

Gather children and talk about the different parts of a book: pages, cover, spine, etc. Have children share their thoughts on how books are made.

Activity

1 To begin making individual books, give each child a sheet of wallpaper or wrapping paper and two sheets of cardboard.

2 Ask children to lay the paper flat and to glue the two cardboard sheets onto it side by side in the center, leaving a ¼" gap between the two. Help children fold and glue the surrounding paper edges onto the cardboard.

3 To make pages for the books, ask each child to fold a pile of three or four sheets of white paper in half, and help children mark six equally spaced dots along the fold. Use a needle to puncture holes for them on the dots. Then give each child a threaded needle to stitch the pages together. (Make sure each end of stitching is tied into a large knot.)

4 Ask children to glue the front and back sheets of their sewn pages onto the inside of the cardboard cover. While the glue dries, talk with children about what they want to write in their books.

Observations

- Do children demonstrate an understanding of the parts of a book?

Books

These stories can enhance children's bookmaking experience.
- *How a Book Is Made* by Aliki (Crowell)
- *I Like Books* by Anthony Browne (Alfred A. Knopf)
- *Too Many Books!* by Caroline F. Bauer (Warne, Frederick & Co.)

SPIN-OFFS

- Talk about publishing. Tell children that the first draft is just for practice. Provide thinking time for children to create a rough plan for their book. After they've thought through their book and made practice copies, have children put a final copy in their cloth-bound book.
- Discuss the function of the title page, including reasons for listing the publisher and copyright date.

Create a Flip Book

Children will "flip" over this activity!

Materials

- 2" x 1" strip of heavy cardboard
- 6" x 10" sheet of construction paper
- crayons and markers
- old magazines
- glue
- scissors
- stapler

Aim

Children will express their ideas as they create and "read" their own book.

In Advance

Ask parents to donate old magazines. Make a flip book yourself as a model.

Activity

1 Discuss the concept of flip books, and talk with children about the types of pictures included in most flip books. Explain that they are usually pictures of familiar things.

2 Ask each child to draw an animal, person, or other familiar thing on a sheet of construction paper or to cut pictures from the magazines to glue onto separate sheets of paper.

3 To make the class flip book, help children stack the pictures into four equal piles and to staple the piles in a row at the top of the cardboard strip, leaving a small space between each pile.

4 Invite children to tell stories using the flip book. Encourage them to "read" a different story each time.

Remember

- Children may find the flip books fascinating. Allow them to create their own individual flip books in a learning center. Stock the center with the necessary materials. You may wish to provide a rebus chart for children on how to assemble a flip book on their own.

Observations

- What kinds of pictures do children draw and cut out? Do they show interest in particular objects or themes?

Books

Reading about these familiar objects might inspire more stories.
- *All Shapes and Sizes* by Shirley Hughes (Lothrop, Lee & Shepard Books)
- *Apples and Pumpkins* by Anne Rockwell (Simon & Schuster)
- *A Children's Zoo* by Tana Hoban (Greenwillow)

SPIN-OFFS

- Help children create flip books that include rows of objects of the same color, shape, or theme that can be matched together.
- Invite each child to make a timeline or sequenced flip book, using photos and drawings of himself or herself at different ages.

Personal Family Books

What's your family like?

Materials

- 8½" x 11" sheets of drawing paper
- plastic report covers (optional)
- transparent tape or glue stick
- photograph of each child's family
- markers
- crayons

Aim

Children will use expressive-language and expository-language skills.

In Advance

Write a letter home asking families to send in a photograph of themselves for a family photo book.

Warm-Up

Invite children to talk about their families and show their family photos. They may like to share their favorite family books, activities, and food.

Activity

1 Set out the drawing paper, markers and crayons, tape or glue, and plastic report covers on your art table. Invite children to make their family books. What might children want to include — drawings of family members, friends, or pets? What will they be doing in the drawing?

2 Take time to discuss ideas as children draw. Ask them to tell you about their pictures, and write down their exact words on a separate sheet of paper.

3 When children are finished, help them slide each page into the plastic report covers. (You can also staple the pages together, but be sure to provide some type of cover for durability.) Encourage children to attach their family photograph to the cover and decorate the cover.

4 Store the family books where children can look at them independently. Throughout the week, take some one-on-one time to read the books with children.

Remember

- Be careful to acknowledge and respect all the different configurations of families.

Observations

- Do children have difficulty talking about their family?

Books

Add these to your bookshelf.
- *Brothers & Sisters* by Ellen B. Senisi (Scholastic Inc.)
- *A Father Like That* by Charlotte Zolotow (Harper & Row)
- *My Mom Travels a Lot* by Caroline Feller Bauer (Penguin Books)

SPIN-OFFS

- Make your family books an ongoing activity. Invite children to add pages to celebrate family events or everyday happenings.
- Children may enjoy this process so much that they would like to make additional books in the same way. Books about grandparents, neighbors, and pets are lots of fun for children to write!

In Our Own Words

Wordless books stimulate language.

Materials

- several wordless books (see suggested titles below) and/or handmade books, plus a few "regular" children's books
- magazines or old children's books
- glue sticks
- drawing paper
- hole punch
- crayons
- long stapler and staples
- string or ribbon
- markers
- camera

Aim

Children will use creative-thinking and writing skills.

Warm-Up

At group time, show children your wordless books. Point out that these are special books everyone can read. Compare the wordless books to other children's books and talk about how they are different.

Activity

1 To create your own wordless books, collect interesting pictures from magazines or old children's books. As you decide on pictures, make sure they progress in a sequence that inspires a story line.

2 Next, help children fold sheets of heavy paper in half. Staple them into a book, or punch holes and tie the sheets together. Then glue the pictures onto the pages.

3 Gather a small group of interested children in a cozy spot. Sit together, hold up one newly created wordless book, and slowly and silently turn the pages. (Children might comment or just look at the pictures.) Now ask children to look at the book again, and this time ask them to make up a story using the pictures.

4 At first, most children will talk about what they actually see on the page. Accept their comments and, at the same time, encourage them to expand their thoughts. You might ask, "What do you think the characters are doing? What do you think they're saying?" After the story is finished, invite the child to choose another wordless book to read. Repeat as long as children remain interested.

Remember

- When choosing wordless books, look for ones with active and engaging pictures that depict an interesting story line.

Observations

- Do children tell the story the same way each time or are there major variations?

Books

Share these wordless books.
- *A Boy, a Dog, and a Friend* by Mercer Meyer (Dial Books)
- *Changes, Changes* by Pat Hutchins (Macmillan)
- *Out! Out! Out!* by Martha Alexander (Dial Books)

SPIN-OFFS

- Create a Book Sharing time! Invite children to read their wordless books with the class. Children may enjoy working in teams to tell their versions of the story.
- If you have a camera, try taking photographs of an event at school or home, and arrange them in sequential order to make a book.

Accordion Books

Here's a fun and easy way to make your own book.

Materials

- 9" x 12" drawing paper
- markers
- crayons
- clear tape

Aim

Children will use creative-thinking, drawing, expressive-language, and writing skills.

Warm-Up

Use the directions below to make your own accordion story. Then share it with children. Remember to keep your book short and simple. Use it to motivate children, not as a model. (It's important to put your book away before you continue with this activity.)

Activity

1 To make an accordion book, help children put two sheets of white paper on top of each other. Fold the pages in half (as if to make a book) and crease them.

2 Next, have children open up the paper and tape one page to the other so that the pages form one long strip.

3 Suggest that children use the creases they created to fold the strip so that it looks like an accordion. Some children might want longer books. To do this, just continue to add pages in a similar manner.

4 Invite children to write and illustrate their books. Keep in mind that there are many ways children can fill their books. Some children will draw or attempt to write words or letters. Still others will want to dictate a story for you to write. Encourage this diversity in style and read each book with equal interest.

Remember

- Some children may not have heard or seen an accordion. Provide photographs and/or recordings of accordions. Ask children what is special about an accordion. Do children see how this musical instrument relates to their books?

Observations

- Do children seem to understand the sequence of the book pages as related to their story?

Books

These are stories where children and books go hand in hand.
- *The Circle Sophie Drew* by Peter and Susan Barrett (Scroll)
- *Happy to Be Me* by Bobbie Kalman (Crabtree)
- *A Picture for Harold's Room* by Crockett Johnson (Harper & Row)

SPIN-OFFS

- Create an Accordion Big Book with full-sized sheets of construction paper and tell a great tale together!
- Encourage children to find other unique books in the classroom book center or their school library. Suggest pop-up books, flip books, and window books. Which books are the children's favorites, and why?

What Comes Next?
Storybooks come complete with captions.

Materials

- large sheet of oaktag folded in half
- black marker
- 1 sheet of drawing paper per child
- markers
- crayons
- paints
- collage materials
- glue
- clear adhesive paper or other laminating material

Aim

Children use listening, speaking, and sequencing skills as they decide what comes first, next, and last in a three-step story.

Warm-Up

At group time, encourage children to talk about their favorite experiences. Help them express their stories sequentially by asking what happened first, next, and last. Have children repeat their stories, adding emphasis to the sequence of events. Then ask the group what happened first, next, and last.

Activity

1 When children share a story they are very excited about, suggest that they make a book together.

2 Help children fold a sheet of drawing paper in half and write the words first, next, and last on the appropriate pages.

3 Ask children to dictate or write what happened first, next, and last. Invite them to choose any art materials they wish to illustrate the book.

4 Encourage children to read their stories to one another at group time. You may want to laminate the book with clear adhesive paper and add it to your library.

Remember

- Offer sequencing opportunities throughout your curriculum. Science and cooking activities lend themselves especially well to first, next, and last steps.

Observations

- Do children use the concepts of first, next, and last in their everyday conversation? How do they understand the sequence?

Books

Share these books about writing and drawing.
- *Fast Draw Freddy* by Bobbie Hamsa (Children's Press)
- *Mouse Writing* by J. Aronsky (Harcourt Brace Jovanovich)
- *Writing and Making Books* by Monica Andrew (Scholastic Inc.)

SPIN-OFFS

- As children become practiced at sequencing three-step stories, help them tell stories in four steps. In four-step sequence stories children can add an extra "next" or a "then" step in the middle of their story.
- Have children create "How to" books in which they illustrate how to do something, such as make a sandwich. Be sure to emphasize sequence.

"My Day" Books

Let's understand the passage of time.

Materials

- experience-chart paper
- construction paper
- magazine pictures
- crayons
- glue
- markers
- stapler
- paper plates
- scissors

Aim

Children will use art, language, writing, and problem-solving skills.

In Advance

Invite children to help you prepare blank "My Day" books.

Warm-Up

Talk about the passage of time. Help children brainstorm a list of all the things they do in the morning. Write these on an experience chart marked with a rising sun (to represent morning). Next, have the children brainstorm all the things they do and see in the afternoon. Use a sun to represent this time of day. Finally, together think of all the things the children do and see at night. Mark this one with a moon or stars. Talk about the similarities and differences in the lists.

Activity

1 Give children their blank "My Day" books and explain that the first page is for the things they do before they come to school. The second page is for what they do during school. The third page is for what they do after school. The fourth page is for their nighttime activities.

2 Provide art materials and magazine pictures for children to work with. Suggest they look for or draw pictures of the things they do at the different times.

3 Encourage them to "write" and draw their thoughts on each page. If they need help, refer to the experience chart. Ask if they would like you to elaborate on the back of each page.

4 Give children time to decorate the covers of their books. Then share the creations.

Observations

- What is the children's understanding of time? Do they use temporal terms correctly?

Books

Share these books with your children.
- *Be Ready at Eight* by Peggy Parish (Macmillan)
- *On Sunday the Wind Came* by Alan C. Elliot (William Morrow & Co.)
- *The Sun's Day* by Mordeicai Richter (HarperCollins)

SPIN-OFFS

- Have children look through magazines for pictures of events that happen throughout a day. Then have them glue or paste the pictures on separate pieces of paper or file cards to form game cards. To play the game, shuffle the cards and encourage children to sequence them from left to right, from morning to night. Ask children to explain the reasoning for their sequence.

Turn Cards Into Books

Here's a fun way to reuse greeting cards.

Materials

- wordless book
- greeting cards
- postcards
- drawing paper
- construction paper
- white glue
- crayons or markers
- stapler

Aim

Children will use creative-thinking and expressive-language skills.

Warm-Up

Ask children to name the different parts of a book, such as pictures, words, pages, and cover. Talk about books that don't have all these parts, such as wordless picture books or novels for adults. Read a wordless book by showing children the pictures and letting them make up the story.

Activity

1 Choose a few of the greeting cards you collected and put them in a sequence. Invite children to help you tell a story the cards create. Then change the sequence or add a few new cards, and make up another story.

2 Let each child choose three or four cards to make up his or her own story. Suggest that children experiment with the sequence of the pictures to create the stories they like best.

3 Pass out drawing paper, glue, and markers or crayons. Children can use these to make the cards into pages for books. Offer colored construction paper for making covers.

4 Help children attach their pages using a stapler or a hole puncher and yarn. Invite children to share their books, one at a time, at meeting time.

Observations

- How closely do children's stories relate to the pictures they choose?

Books

These wordless books will make good models for children as they create their own books.

- *Changes, Changes* by Pat Hutchins (Macmillan)
- *Do You Want to Be My Friend?* by Eric Carle (Putnam)
- *The Grey Lady and the Strawberry Snatcher* by Molly Bang (Four Winds Press)
- *Pancakes for Breakfast* by Tomie dePaola (Harcourt Brace Jovanovich)
- *Three Cats* by Anne Brouillard (Thomasson-Grant)

SPIN-OFFS

- Recycled holiday cards are also good for sewing activities. Punch holes around the edges, and let children weave yarn through the holes.
- Each day, focus on a few of the stories children have written. Encourage each "author" to share his book with the group. Pass the books around so the children can see them up close. The books make great gifts for family and friends!

It's Nice to Remember

Save the memories of wonderful times.

Materials

- camera and film
- construction paper
- pencils
- blank photo album
- heavy white drawing paper
- crayons and markers
- pens

Aim

Children will use expressive-, receptive-, and creative-language skills, as well as creative-thinking, reading, and writing skills.

In Advance

Bring in a yearbook or photo album to share. Also, ask a family member to be a roving "candid camera" person in your class. Make sure that everyone is in at least a few of the pictures.

Warm-Up

Encourage children to talk about the events of the year and the things they enjoyed, learned, and remember. Encourage children to talk about which trips, games, centers, and snacks they liked best. Make a list entitled "Our Best Memories," and invite children to illustrate.

Activity

1 After you have developed the pictures, gather children to show them the yearbook you've brought in. Tell them that one way people remember the fun they had together is to make a book about it. Point out various photographs of people and the writing that describes what is happening or tells something about the person.

2 Show the developed photographs, and allow plenty of time for children to look at and discuss the pictures. After children have enjoyed the pictures say, "We can use these pictures to make our own yearbook."

3 Help children choose pictures and decide what they want to say about themselves and the year. Encourage them to tell about the things they liked, their friends, what they remember best, and so on. They can either write using invented spelling or dictate their ideas.

4 Give children paper to paste their pictures and their stories on. They can also add decorations. Then slip the papers into the magnetic pages of an inexpensive photo album to officially "publish" the book. Each child can take home his or her own original page.

Observations

- What is the content of children's writings? Do they tell what they see in the picture or tell about the event?

Books

Here are some books about children and school.
- *Bea and Mrs. Jones* by Amy Schwartz (Bradbury Press)
- *Best Friends* by Miriam Cohen (Macmillan)
- *Timothy Goes to School* by Rosemary Wells (Dial)

SPIN-OFFS

- If possible, photocopy all the pages of the book, and staple them together to make a take-home yearbook for each child. Make photocopies for children to take home.
- Suggest that children make an album of their summer break. Remind them that drawings of their activities are another way to keep memories alive.

Once Upon a Big Book

Turn a favorite song into an original story.

Materials

- large sheets of paper
- markers or crayons
- large piece of cardboard or posterboard
- hole puncher
- fasteners

Aim

Children will use imaginative-thinking and cooperative skills to create a book together.

Warm-Up

Read or sing a book based on one of your group's favorite songs. (See suggestions below.) Invite children to make up a few new verses. For example, if you read *Over in the Meadow*, they might add a verse about a goat or a dinosaur. Explain that they can make a Big Book of their made-up song.

Activity

1 Use large chart paper to record children's ideas for new verses. Set out large sheets of paper and markers or crayons for children to make the pages of their book.

2 Help each child decide which page he or she wants to make for the book. Some children might want to work together. Encourage children to talk out their ideas as they illustrate their pages.

3 After making their drawings, children may dictate their ideas or use invented spelling to write their verses.

4 Ask children to decide together on a title for their book, and point out that they are the authors. Invite everyone interested to help make the cover out of cardboard or posterboard. Attach the pages and cover together. Display the book where children can read it independently.

Remember

- Some children may prefer to write and draw a real verse from a song rather than invent a new one.

Observations

- How much do children talk and cooperate as they work on their book? What language skills are evident?

Books

Here are a few books based on songs.
- *Alligators All Around* by Maurice Sendak (HarperCollins)
- *Over in the Meadow* by David Carter (Scholastic Inc.)
- *This Old Man* by Carol Jones (Houghton Mifflin)

SPIN-OFFS

- Invite children to create their own version of another favorite storybook. Use the same approach of reading the story first and brainstorming ideas for changing or continuing the story. Try books such as *If the Dinosaurs Came Back* by Bernard Most (Harcourt Brace Jovanovich) or *Animals Should Definitely Not Wear Clothing* by Judi Barrett (Simon & Schuster).